the CHAP

MANIFESTO

REVOLUTIONARY ETIQUETTE
FOR THE MODERN GENTLEMAN

4th

FOURTH ESTATE
LONDON

GUSTAV TEMPLE & VIC DARKWOOD

CONFEDERACY OF ANARCHO-DANDYISTS

FIRST PUBLISHED IN GREAT BRITAIN IN 2001
BY FOURTH ESTATE
A DIVISION OF HARPERCOLLINSPUBLISHERS
77-85 FULHAM PALACE ROAD
LONDON W6 8JB

WWW.4THESTATE.CO.UK

A CATALOGUE RECORD FOR THIS BOOK IS AVAILABLE FROM THE BRITISH LIBRARY.

ISBN 1-84115-657-4

DESIGNED BY M2 / PRINTED BY THE BATH PRESS LTD, BATH.

 A CALL TO CHARMS

CHUMRADES...

FOR TOO LONG we have been the playthings of massive corporations, whose sole aim is to convert our world into a gargantuan shopping 'mall'. Pleasantry and civility are being discarded as the worthless ephemera of a bygone age; an age when men doffed their hats at ladies, and children could be counted on to mind your Jack Russell while you took a mild and bitter in the pub. The twinkly-eyed tobacconist, the ruddy-cheeked pub landlord and the bewhiskered teashop lady are being trampled under the mighty blandness of 'drive-thru' hamburger chains. Customers are herded in and out of such places with an alarming similarity to the way the cattle used to produce the burgers are herded to the slaughterhouse.

The principal victim of this blandification is Youth, whose natural propensity to shun work, peacock around the town and aggravate the constabulary has been drummed out of them. Youth is left with a sad deficiency of *joie de vivre*, imagination and elegance. Instead, their lives are ruled by territorial one-upmanship based on brands of plimsoll, and Youth has become little more than a walking, barely talking advertising hoarding for global conglomerates.

And what has Youth got to look forward to? The life of the *lumpen officetariat* consists of toiling away all day in front of computer screens, transferring swathes of dull information from one terminal to another. In their spare time, they are to be found at large halls of misery, where chemically-laden beer is fed to them while they ogle sport events on larger versions of the same screens they have been staring at all day. The resulting 'culture' of this state of affairs can be summed up in one word: vulgarity. In short, society as a whole is being crushed under the oppressive weight of a ruling *vulgaroisie*.

But now, a spectre is beginning to haunt the reigning vulgaroisie: the spectre of Chappism. A new breed of insurgent has begun to appear on the streets, in the taverns and in the offices of Britain: the Anarcho-Dandyist. Recognisable by his immaculate clothes, the rakish angle of his hat and his subtle rallying cry of "Good day to you sir/madam!"

This seemingly quaint and harmless individual has also been spotted in small groups on the fringes of contemporary protest gatherings, in cities as remote from civilised life as Seattle and Kyoto. While straggly-haired youths in balaclavas shout slogans and smash the windows of McDonald's, the Anarcho-Dandyists merely display the razor-sharp creases on their moleskin trousers, arching an eyebrow over their monocles with a wry smile.

It is time for the Confederacy of Anarcho-Dandyists (CAD) to publish their views, their aims and their tenets. By uniting the various strands of Chappist agit-fop under one ensign, we will prevent the inevitable fragmentation that afflicts all ideological struggles. Thus The Chap Manifesto will serve as a blueprint for the Charmed Uprising, and unite all gentlemanly insurgents to ensure the victory of the Tweed Revolution.

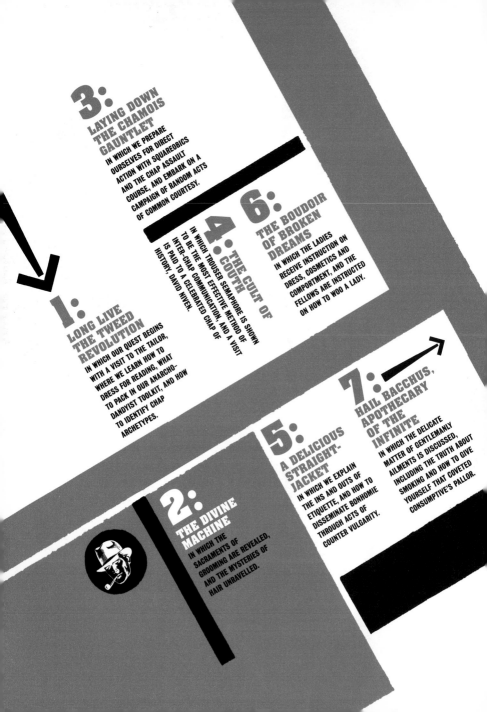

CONTENTS

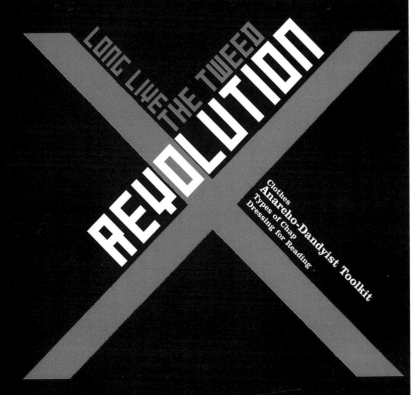

LONG LIVE THE TWEED

REVOLUTION

Clothes
Anarcho-Dandyist Toolkit
Types of Chap
Dressing for Reading

Urban Outwitter
Essential Raiment for the Revolutionary Dandy

The four-in-hand is a perfectly adequate knot for a morning stroll, but for intensive Anarcho-Dandyist activity you should consider something more radical, such as a **Windsor knot.**

Not only are **cufflinks** *a badge of honour worn upon the sleeve, they are also the only item of jewellery a gentleman is permitted, and therefore a splendid mode of self-expression.*

"Black shoes go with everything," is the preposterous cry heard in shoe shops across the land. They do not. **Brown shoes** *and tweed suits are as inseparable as roast beef and mustard or gin and tonic.*

Separate collars *will separate you from the common herd, who can barely manage to fasten their velcro, let alone master the intricacies of a collar stud.*

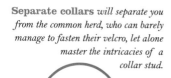

Braces, *as opposed to belts, provide adequate support for the trousers, while allowing the wearer to over indulge at lunch without having to loosen anything.*

Full-length underwear *should not be overlooked when dressing in tweed. The skin will need protection from some of the rougher thornproofs, which are usually only partly lined.*

The Anarcho-Dandyist Toolkit

Items to Conceal About Your Person when Sallying Forth into the Public Arena

Scented handkerchief. *This will beam positive messages to any ladies you encounter. The delicate fragrances of bergamot and frangipani will put them at their ease, assuring them that they are not in the menacing presence of a testosterone-heavy male.*

Nail scissors. *This multi-facetted tool can be adapted from its customary role as a grooming aid and be employed in snipping the wires of personal stereos on public transport (see* Random Acts of Common Courtesy*).*

Hairdryer with shoulder holster. *Spend as much time as possible loitering in workplace lavatories warming seats to temperatures more suited to leisurely evacuation. This ruse will encourage fellow employees to dally in cubicular confinement for hours on end, thus undermining the very foundation of the corporate power structure (see* The Shirk Ethic*).*

Lighter on a pulley. *Should you find yourself sequestered by villains and tied up in a chair, a sliding lighter concealed under your sleeve might serve to ignite your captor's cigar at a crucial moment, thus avoiding a dreadful faux pas.*

Sock suspenders. *No man of substance would ever countenance leaving his home without ensuring that his socks were in a state of firm equilibrium, but these stylish requisites may also be converted in a trice into a multitude of items such as a makeshift slingshot or garrotte, or a sturdy fan belt replacement.*

Blakeys. *A simple expedient to warn any loitering ruffians of your impending approach. The metallic tap-tap of your heels will alert all to the fact that you are a man of substance and panache and therefore not to be trifled with.*

The Gang of Four

IF YOU ARE INTENT on participating in the Tweed Revolution yet find yourself stumbling in the mists of sartorial uncertainty, you may find it useful to examine the four essential types of Chap. You should find that your physiognomy, character and dress sense fit snugly into the mould of one of the four splendid fellows illustrated here.

1. The Dandy

 The Dandy is the highest form of existence attainable by the human form. His life is exclusively dedicated to dressing exquisitely, parading about the fashionable boroughs of splendid cities and holding forth at his club, where he dispenses witticism as readily as the vulgaroisie utters its banal platitudes. The only species of 'work' this singular Chap might engage in would consist of discussing buttonhole stitching with his tailor and performing his ablutions until the morning has been well aired enough for him to step into it.

2. The Cad

 Also known as the rogue, the bounder and the absolute rotter, this fellow devotes his life to breaking the hearts of pretty ladies. However, he always manages to dispense such pleasure, before the inevitable fissure, that most ladies are glad to have spent even a short time in his thrilling world. The Cad will transport the ladies into previously unchartered territories of sophistication and pleasure in the passenger seat of his sleek open-top sports car, before depositing them, still weak at the knees with giddy satiation, back at the suburban nests of their flabby little husbands.

3. The Hearty Fellow

 Like a fine malt whisky matured in an oak cask, the Hearty Fellow has supped at the grand table of Dionysus and thoroughly enjoyed it, yet he is still at his peak. You will find him in country inns, sampling the joys of the local ale, which he always takes in a dimpled pint glass and never a straight one. The Hearty Fellow's leisure pursuits may include chairmanship of a Chappist club or association, such as a moustache-growers' club or a pipe-smokers' council. He applies his drinking principles to his every activity, so nothing is done in half measures. Not for him is the hirsute flippancy of a pencil moustache; the hearty fellow will sport upper lip shrubbery of such magnificence that grown men will weep when beholding it.

4. The Poet

 Ah, the poet! What sweetness is his misery, what joy his pain! He is the master of the overstatement, living his life as if it were a continual sonnet to beauty, sadness and despair. The poet is the prima donna of his own perpetual one-act tragedy. Where the vulgaroisie find pleasure and satisfaction, he finds nothing more than a shallow mockery of desire. The poet enjoys nothing more than to languish on a chaise longue all afternoon, wistfully reciting Coleridge and Chatterton while a sympathetic sister plucks a melancholic ballad on a guitar.

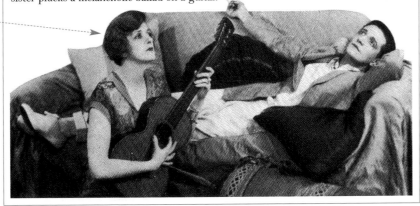

Dressing for Reading

THE FOUNDATIONS OF the Tweed Revolution are carved from the bedrock of literature. It is therefore incumbent upon a fellow to dress appropriately for the study of Chappist literature. One cannot very well approach Baudelaire dressed in jeans and plimsolls. The dandy poet would turn in his grave at the very thought. Similarly, Blake would expect us to settle down with his works in nothing more restrictive than a loose robe, or preferably naked. Here are some suggested outfits to don while you hone your mind to a fine instrument of insurgency within the snug confines of your library.

Above: *Woollen dressing gown, silk pyjamas, velvet slippers*
Reading matter:
In Search of Comfort: Comte Fragonard de Languidere
The Hurly Burly of the Chaise Longue: Fiona Salter
Breakfast at Sundown: Torquil Eiderdown

Right: *Beige linen suit, white shirt, yellow silk tie,*
Panama hat, white canvas naval shoes
Reading matter:
The Pleasures of Istanbul: Lord Marmaduke Ficklepants-Watt
Fields of Dreams, Meadows of Vice: Monty Cantsin
I Wore My Linen Trousers: Basil Collier

Top: *White cotton kefir, embroidered Persian slippers, Moroccan fez*

Reading matter:

The Cabbala: Anon

The Baghavad-Gita: Anon

The Book of the Law: Aleister Crowley

Left: *Tweed plus fours, white cotton shirt, yellow moleskin waistcoat, woollen 8-section cap*

Reading matter:

O'er Hill and Yonder Dale:
Brigadier Henry St Wittermaster

The Delights of Breeding Voles:
Solomon Crabtree-Spatt

Links I Have Loved: Sheridan Fairweather

THE
DIVINE
MACHINE

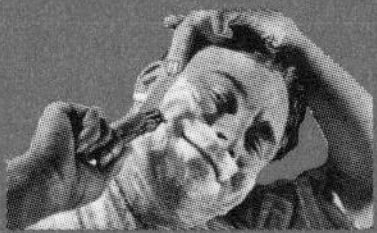

THE SEMIOTICS OF HAIR

GROOMING

The Philosophy of Grooming

WE ARE BORN virtually hairless. Once an obliging midwife has swabbed the uterial slime off us and given us a reviving slap on the backside, we enter the world with a smooth, peachy complexion. But, as we grow older, the ravages of existence take their toll on our skin and our hair embarks on its own peculiar journey through growth, greyness and fallout, not necessarily in that order. George Orwell was of the opinion that by the time a man reaches 30, he has the face he deserves. Judging from the few photographs that exist of Mr Orwell, he did not deserve very much. But he did have a point. If we are to devote ourselves to the Chappist life from early adolescence, with a daily breakfast of devilled kidneys, an hourly cup of strong, sweet tea, 60 Capstan Navy Cut cigarettes, a martini at 5, a G&T at 6, a bottle of *vin fin* with dinner, several post-prandial absinthes and a malt whisky at midnight, as well as a large portion of our time spent in smoky hostelries and gambling houses, then we jolly well deserve to resemble WH Auden with a bad case of flu.

So why do we not, gentlemen? What is the secret we harbour, which allows us to maintain the complexion of a babe in arms while living the life of Dorian Gray? The answer is, of course, grooming. For though we may shirk from our supposed duties in the workplace, and though we may suddenly have a pressing engagement to attend when confronted by a pub bully, when it comes to grooming we are men of courage and action. We brandish our cut-throat razors like the swords of destiny to vanquish our follicular foes. Our tubs of macassar are like phials of holy oil to be used in magical rites and incantations. For a gentleman, there is no area more sacred than "that place whereat he shall groom himself" (Ablutions, 5:14). It doesn't matter if that place is a marble-topped dressing table with a gilded mirror in a Berkshire mansion, or a chipped sink and a fragment of broken mirror in the corner of a bedsit. With a few essential requisites, any such space can be converted into a sacred grooming altar.

The Sacraments of Grooming

While showers are an excellent way of getting to know your privates during military service, they are not appropriate for civilian life. A daily bath, taken immediately after a hearty breakfast, is an excellent way to mull over the tasks ahead – even if those tasks consist of lounging about the house all day in a dressing gown. After an hour or two in the bath, your pores should be open and your follicles primed for pruning. By now bathroom visibility will be at a minimum, and you won't be able to see anything at all in the mirror, let alone enough to scrape a cut-throat razor across your face. A surprising, and very useful, chemical reaction seems to occur between the smoke produced by pipe tobacco and bathroom steam. Have a puff or two on your briar and watch the steam miraculously clear, like the dawn mist lifting off the Amazon.

The Big Shave

The difference between proper shaving soap and air-compressed foams is like comparing freshly made Italian ice cream to Mr Whippy. Shaving soap comes in attractive wooden bowls, or in discreet stick form. Both products are a welcome addition to the grooming altar and both can be worked into a superb meringue-like lather with a badger-hair brush. Once you have completed your shave (always against the direction of hair growth, of course) wash off the lather and inspect your face for cuts. If there are any, simply get into your pyjamas and go back to bed, for God has decreed that you shall not leave the house today.

Next, we must approach the unappealing matter of unwanted facial hair outside the remit of your razor. The Turks, without doubt the grooming masters of the world (if you can get yourself a Turkish barber, you are set up for a luxurious life of grooming ease), have a novel method of removing nasal hair. They insert a thin wax taper into each nostril, then set it alight. In a second the tiny hairs are exterminated, leaving delightfully clear air passages through which to enjoy the sensual aromas of the Turkish barbershop.

A Glossary of Sheens

The various hairstyle options are outlined in the next section. Maintenance of these barnets is another matter entirely. Rule number one is: no matter what style you choose to configure your hair into, the hair itself should always be shiny. Shiny hair and shiny shoes, covering as they do the essential extremities of a chumrade, consolidate the notion of a highly polished revolutionary unit, demonstrating to the scruffy vulgaroisie that Chappism is not here to take any prisoners. Just make sure you do not mix up your brushes and get Brylcreem all over your brogues.

Having said that, there are several options available to the impecunious gent who finds himself with a paucity of pomade. Salvador Dali's early experiments with dandyism in 20s Madrid saw him plastering his abundant barnet with furniture polish, which set into a species of mahogany coffee table on his head. We can only bow to such hirsute dedication, and humbly offer the following alternatives to real pomade. Boot blacking mixed with olive oil gets up a nice sheen, as does a wad of lard infused with gravy browning. The latter is not suitable for vegetarians.

Gentlemanly Requisites
The Bare Essentials for a Chap's Grooming Altar

Morgan's Pomade *colours greying locks and enables you to sculpt your hair into a variety of pleasing pompadour effects.*

The Solida 'Lord' Gent's Hairdressing Cap. *Especially recommended for the man too busy or just too idle to carry a comb.*

Pinaud 'Clubman' Moustache Wax *acts as a follicular viagra promoting uplifting self-confidence and lasting sub-nasal erectitude.*

Arko Shaving Soap *ensures that your razor's encounters with your chin proceed with smoothness and accuracy.*

Klippette Nasal Hair Clippers. *Effective in the removal of unsightly and embarrassing nasal shrubbery.*

The Cut-Throat Razor. *Essential for experienced groomers with a penchant for living on the edge.*

The Semiotics of Hair

IN THE REVOLUTIONARY STRUGGLE that lies ahead it would be wise for all gents to put aside an evening or two to gen up on the teachings of those grand masters of semiotics, Ferdinand de Saussure, Umberto Eco and Roland Barthes. These outstandingly clever coves knew a thing or two when it came to reading and interpreting signs and symbols, and when their methods are applied to the arena of hairstyles they can provide a chap with a very powerful tool for spotting the difference on the street between chumrade or scoundrel. Not surprisingly, there is still a strong trend in English thinking that sees such methodology as so much continental tommyrot. However, a few brief days out in the 'field' should be enough to convince even the most hardened sceptic of the acute psychological insight that might be gained from the calm and objective appraisal of a man's coiffure. When a fellow walks into a barber's shop and demands a particular follicular configuration, he brings with him the psychic baggage of his hopes, fears, loves and disappointments. The plumage that he chooses to exhibit upon his bonce can be as telling and as individual as his genetic make-up, his fingerprints or the contents of his trouser pockets.

The Renaissance

A bald pate exhibited with confidence and pride singles out a man as both honourable and dignified. Coupled with ferociously luxuriant beard growth, potential suitors are left in no doubt about complete satisfaction in the cantilever department.

The Mexican

A chap wishing to appear somewhat devil-may-care and risqué may find himself drawn inexorably towards the jaunty 'Mexican', now sadly annexed by bier-keller volken, middle-aged homosexuals, Australian cricketers and persons from Stockport.

The Handlebar

This cove's dapper facial attire reinforces his reputation as a great humanitarian and philanthropist, gained through many years of sterling work, helping young bedouin boys out of the Moroccan gutter and into his Mayfair apartment.

The Scalp String

By wantonly indulging in a ludicrous practice known as 'scalp-stringing', this man vainly attempts to turn back the ravages of time and appear dynamic and sporty. He is guilty of the worst kind of naivity and self-deception.

The Dandelion

This boffin's late night liaisons with test tube and Bunsen burner leave him with little time to dally with the concept of 'style'. A mind firmly set on lofty ideals and transcendent notions is as often as not accompanied by a coiffure of abject foolishness.

The Skinhead

Surely this chump needs a new barber. A la mode with Russian dissidents in the 30s and 40s, right-wing 'youth' in the 70s and would-be bohemians in the 90s, this anti-hairstyle is now far too widespread and popular to have any true meaning at all.

The Majestic

Even denuded of his Gieves and Hawkes suit and Lobb Oxfords, this fine cove could be forgiven for claiming to be fully dressed. Where the grand and questing 'Majestic' precedes, a thoroughly decent fellow is bound to follow.

The Goatee

This cheeky Gallic tuft portrays an independence of judgement and a singularity of spirit. Sadly degraded these days in its usage by jazz musicians and popular entertainers, who overly prune back their beards to the merest designer stubble.

The Rebel

This young turk shows a charming hint of rebellion that is both desirable and attractive in teenage years. But his father watches him carefully, as too voluptuous a use of brilliantine may harbinger a penchant for rock 'n' roll, brawling and satanism.

The Chiff-chafro

Not satisfied by the political integrity of the stylish 'Afro', this man has allowed his interests in ornithology and topiary to lead him to the point of buffoonery. It should be remembered that simplicity and understatement are their own rewards.

The Bombardier

The 15th Earl of Camarthenshire is apt to be somewhat 'creative' and 'theatrical' at the best of times. The adoption of a 'Bombardier' as a manly facial ornament is a welcome indication that he is at last preparing to travel a route of moral rectitude.

The Rococo

One of the unfortunate side effects of accumulating obscene amounts of lucre at an early age, through a career in popular music, is a tendency in later life to make up for waning creative powers through increasingly desperate facial hair statements.

The Mullet

This fellow is quite simply guilty of a coiffure unbefitting of a gentleman. It is, however, somewhat more acceptable in Scandinavia, where a cold climate and excessive drinking render normal modes of aesthetic judgement impossible.

The Periwig

Good God! What can be the meaning of such knavery? Even the most subtle attempts at concealing baldness are blatantly apparent to the practised eye. This fellow-m'lad is fooling no one but himself. Watch out baldy, the joke's on you.

LAYING DOWN THE CHAMOIS GAUNTLET

Squaerobics
Chap Assault Course
Random Acts of Common Courtesy
Tipping

Squaerobics

THERE ARE FEW THINGS more deplorable to a man of worth than physical exercise, but still the myth is perpetuated, by press and government alike, that dressing up in flamboyantly coloured nylon clothing, indecently tight lycra and other charmless sportswear whilst indulging in a mindless regimen of punishing jerks and unnatural bending are practices that should be actively encouraged. We are subjected to endless sloganising, such as "Give it 101%" and "No pain, no gain", when it seems patently obvious that giving 60% is usually more than adequate to achieve most tasks and that pain, outside the confines of the bed chamber, is very unpleasant indeed.

Nevertheless, whilst earnestly exhorting you to avoid exercise if you possibly can, the Confederacy of Anarcho-Dandyists (CAD) reluctantly acknowledges that there are those among us who find themselves in possession of an overly energetic disposition, and who find it impossible to curb their lust for physical recreation. Squaerobics has been developed for just this sort of person, allowing exercise to be entered into whilst at the same avoiding the shameful reputation that naturally connects itself to such unsavoury urges. This is achieved

by the use of a series of camouflage tactics utilising the inconspicuous nature of daily household rituals to cover up a regular fitness routine. As a result, the streets of our cities will gradually be swept clear of the vulgar display of grown men and women disporting themselves in the most disreputable manner.

Exercise 1
Infant Elevating
Squaerobics puts an end to the age-old philosophical conundrum, "What are babies are actually for?"
Whilst playing the dutiful uncle, the nearest available infant may be utilised in the manner shown in order to render the deltoids spick and span.

Exercise 2
Dropping Things
This fellow might be regarded, by the hoi polloi, as a blundering oaf. Their prejudice blinds them to the fact that continual dropping of pipes and other personal equipment presents a marvellous opportunity for exercising the muscles of the lower back region.

Exercise 3
Listening
Attending tea parties at one's maiden aunt's can be a pretty gruelling affair especially when interminable tittle-tattle is entered into. Feigning wide-eyed appreciation of an amusing tale and leaning close can do wonders for the intercostal muscles.

Exercise 4
The Pre-prandial Clench
The aeons that elapse between the sounding of the dinner gong and actual serving of the food may be profitably spent in a rigorous working of the trapezii and latissimus dorsi. Fellow guests will put your rigid posture down to a keen Pavlovian anticipation. ☞

Exercise 5
Reading Poetry

Voracious consumption of Parnassian poetry and decadent literature is renowned for its ability to make one irresistible to the ladies. It is less well known that it can also provide a jolly decent workout for the pectorals and deltoids.

Exercise 6
Comedy

Imitating the ludicrous in-flight safety demonstrations of aeroplane staff is virtually guaranteed to have fellow guests at a party falling off their seats with mirth. Your popularity and the definition of your back muscles will burgeon in consequence.

Exercise 7
Music

The heady Latin rhythms of South America can induce a fellow to throw all caution to the wind and gyrate his pelvis shamelessly. Getting one's hands on a fine pair of maracas will do wonders for the cardiovascular system.

Exercise 8
Scurf Brushing
The advent of central heating has resulted in an epidemic of dandruff in offices across the nation. No one will bat an eyelid at this jaunty, twin-handed brushing technique which cleverly doubles up as a most efficacious workout of the biceps.

Exercise 9
At the Art Gallery
Thanks to the confounding nature of modern art, the gallery has now become the ideal environment for removing fat build-up around the external oblique muscles. Twist your upper torso and head from side to side as if straining for aesthetic enlightenment.

Exercise 10
The Yo-Yo
Dismissed by some as a trivial child's game, the yo-yo is rapidly gaining Olympic sports status among those in the know. Five minutes of vigorous undulation, morning and evening, will have you as nimble and perky as a squirrel in springtime.

The Anarcho-Dandyist Assault Course

The first stage of training, at Brogue Camp, Pimlico, pits our recruits against some typical challenges they will face in the modern world.

1. Fast Food Outlet
Go into a branch of McDonald's and order a dry Martini made to your exact specifications: ten parts Gordons Gin, a single sunbeam directed through a bottle of vermouth, and one Andalucian olive.

2. High Street Chain Store
Ask to speak to the head cutter. When told that no such staff member exists, ask for your suit measurements to be taken by a charming young counter assistant.

3. Chain Pub
Enter a branch of All Bar One wearing red fez, silk pyjamas and dressing gown. Order glass of port, plate of stilton and Turkish boy to light cigar.

HAZARD

VULGAR YOUTH

4. Trendy Nightclub
During a 'Garage' night at 'Home', persuade all the punters to join you in the garage of your own home. Enchant them with some of your own 'phat flavas' by that sublime old phellow, Noel Coward.

Random Acts of Common Courtesy

ANY GENT READING THIS MANIFESTO for the first time may initially find himself horror-struck at the notion of insurrection and the charmed uprising. "Surely," he will conjecture "such social upheaval will require me to tumble out of bed afore noon and indulge in all sorts of energetic pursuits." We of the CAD understand your concerns, but wish to reassure you that capturing the hearts and minds of your fellow man will merely entail a stepping up of any gentleman's customary code of daily civility. Come join us on a concerted campaign of random acts of common courtesy. Take up your kid-leather gloves and brolly, and try out the practical, no nonsense strategies outlined below.

At Home

The home is the ideal environment for developing and honing the skills necessary to realising our subversive goals. Practice and preparation here will reap dividends later on, when confronted with opposition in the 'real world' of the office and the street.

To begin with, it is recommended that a good many hours are spent standing before the glass perfecting a demeanour of exquisite imperturbability. If you are feeling particularly adventurous, why not try clouding your brow with sweet mystery or allowing the merest hint of a knowing smile play upon your lips. It should be remembered that faced with ridicule or attack these are your most effective weapons. Savoir-faire to a gentleman is as the trusty kalashnikov to an Afghan rebel. Maintain it well and use it wisely and it will look after you in return.

But now to practical matters. Your initial tentative forays into 'making a difference' may be fraught with nervousness and self-doubt. If this is likely to be the case, don't overstretch yourself at first. Start off gently. For example, if you live in rooms that form part of a multi-occupied building, take to lurking in the shadows of communal stairways. On hearing approaching footfalls, dart from your chosen hiding place and greet passers-by with a hearty "Good day to you, Sir." or a slightly more winsome, "May I extend my hand in your general direction?"

Having conquered your fears and the hearts and minds of your neighbours, it might be time to escalate action somewhat. In the general vicinity of your abode there will almost inevitably live a little old lady. To the aggressive, ambitious and the terminally employed, little old ladies will symbolise wasted tax revenue and an unwanted reminder of the crepe-fleshed horror of mortality. But, oh no, not to the likes of us. On the contrary. For those of discernment and style, the little old lady is a symbol of the meek harmony of the universe and an untapped human resource. Under correct supervision, these small, frail, pitiful creatures can once again be allowed to feel useful and wanted. Pay a visit to a little old lady near you, furnish her with a list of your comestible requirements and point her in the

general direction of Fortnum & Mason, J. Sainsbury, Waitrose or some other grocer of note. The carrying of heavily laden shopping bags is scientifically proven to be invaluable in the augmentation of flagging muscle tone and self-esteem in the elderly.

In the Street

Whilst walking through the street you will come into close contact with 'the enemy'. That is, the hoi poloi indulging in all sorts of jostling, rudery and unpleasantness in order to gain a march on their fellow man. Even though sorely provoked you should never allow yourself to lose your temper or retaliate. Restraint is all. Timing must be impeccable. Darting nimbly in and out of the crowd, throw yourself into a frenzy of random hat raising, tossing a cheery quip here and a more substantial bon mot there, show them that we mean business and are prepared to take no prisoners.

You will notice as you glide on your trajectory that many of the enemy will be sporting that ignoble instrument of shame, the mobile phone. Whilst this unspeakable affectation is rumoured to be growing in popularity it is nonetheless infra dig with all those dedicated to politesse, serenity and beauty of mind. With this aforethought, it is incumbent upon you to be proficient in the disabling of cellular technology. To these ends, a light but stout hammer should be carried at all times and particular attention should be paid to Fig. 1 which illustrates the most effective dual-blow technique for the dispatching of irritatingly insistent phone ringing. Accurately applied pin-point strikes at points A and B should be enough to silence even the most robust brands of phone. By dispensing summary justice in this way to the mongers of discord and discourtesy you will gain the gratitude and respect of all right-thinking people.

As you progress down the public byways of town or country there will be the odd occasion when you chance upon the lost property of some hapless individual or other. This may take the form of a small trinket of jewellery, a heftily furnished wallet or a dainty morsel of ladies' underwear. Whatever it may be, modern revolutionary etiquette stipulates that if the found item is not accompanied by identification, then it is entirely within the judgement of the finder as to whether or not to hand it in to the constabulary. As a rough guide, it should be pointed out that any object that is plainly of no intrinsic worth, for example, base metal or plastic jewellery, is probably the property of a person of meagre

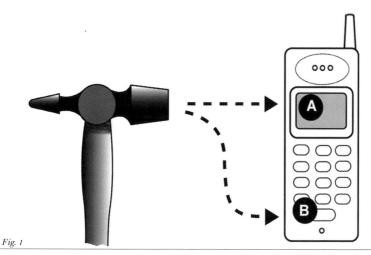

Fig. 1

means and therefore it would be a kindness to hand the article in forthwith. On the other hand, precious metals and large rolls of crisp bank notes in all likelihood belong to someone of sanguine finance and consequently maybe kept with a clear conscience. In the happy instance of a name or address accompanying the found item, the above rule applies but it is rigorously enforced by common courtesy that the beneficiary of the find should write to the original owner of the found article thanking them kindly for their largesse and explaining the particular circumstances that have led to the decision (Fig. 2).

As an *agent raconteur*, when called into action you must be ready and willing to inflict cordiality and harmony at the drop of a well-brushed fedora. Circumstances are bound to arise that will involve thinking on your feet and responding to challenge swiftly, yet with grace and dignity. Take, for example, the situation where you find yourself engrossed in conversation in a public telephone booth and you become aware of a member of the public standing impatiently outside awaiting their turn. The usual response would be to turn one's back and pretend that you are blissfully unaware of their presence, but it takes only a little nous and initiative to turn inconvenience into serendipity. Fling open the door, smile rakishly and invite your guest to join in a jaunty téléphonage-a-trois.

On Public Transport

The soaring temperatures of high summer can often act as a catalyst to man's uncourtliness to man. This is nowhere more apparent than on the bus, train or tube, where vomiting children, body odour and shell suits can result in patience wearing thin.

A few well thought-out strategies and a handful of dedicated *agents raconteurs*, can rescue this seemingly lost situation and make travelling by public transport an almost tolerable experience.

On boarding, it is essential that a skilled agent immediately secures the trust and respect of his fellow passengers and the transport staff. This may be done in a number of ways

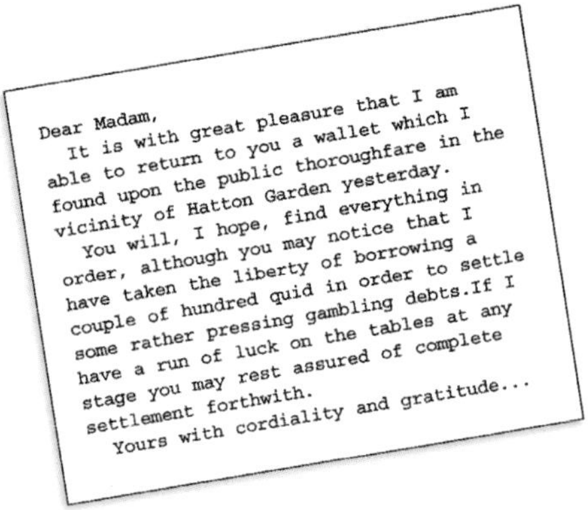

Dear Madam,
It is with great pleasure that I am able to return to you a wallet which I found upon the public thoroughfare in the vicinity of Hatton Garden yesterday.
You will, I hope, find everything in order, although you may notice that I have taken the liberty of borrowing a couple of hundred quid in order to settle some rather pressing gambling debts. If I have a run of luck on the tables at any stage you may rest assured of complete settlement forthwith.
Yours with cordiality and gratitude...

Fig. 2

ranging from a simple, "May I convey to you my hearty regards, madam," to the more physical approach of lightly placing your hand on the forearm of the person next to you, whilst leaning face to face and beaming a smile of the most ferocious intensity.

The loyalty of transport staff can be secured by the simple expedient of tipping the conductor on payment of one's fare. However, it is essential that such an exchange is carried out with modesty and aplomb, as ostentatious largesse will only single you out as smug and condescending. (See section on Tipping)

As you relax into your role you will find you are able to take more affirmative action. For example, little old ladies often fall prey to well-meaning individuals who ghetto-ise them by forcing them to sit in OAP designated areas. This is not only humiliating but it has also been proven that lengthy sitting greatly increases the likelihood of osteoporosis, thrombosis and haemorrhoids in the elderly. Using an appropriate lure, such as packet of lemon bon-bons, a bottle of Babycham or an unfinished piece of crochet work, usher the little old lady to the nearest standing rail and, sitting yourself down in her newly vacated place, proudly observe the consequent burgeoning of her physical health and mental well-being.

Overly crowded carriages and buses can provide particularly fertile areas of covert operation. It may take some practice and determination to function efficiently in such trying conditions but the potential rewards are great. Take, for example, that bane of civilised tranquillity, the personal stereo. This object of infamy is becoming alarmingly prevalent on all modes of transport but only becomes truly offensive when, due to the immoderacy of the listener, the volume is pumped up to a generally audible percussive hiss. Using the sinuous stealth of the puma, undulate your way through the throng and insinuate yourself into a position adjacent to the offender. Do not make eye contact. Remain dignified and erect. In the palm of your hand you will have secreted a small pair of nail scissors. These should be utilised in the manner illustrated in Figure 3. It is highly recommended that you make your strike shortly before your transport reaches a stop, as you will be able to make a swift getaway before your victim has worked out exactly what has happened.

In an age that has steadily undermined a man's fundamental right to smoke, transport authorities have meekly followed suit, cynically bringing in legislation that dehumanises their passengers and seeks to convert them into obedient automaton clones. To re-establish our self-volition and amour propre, whilst at the same time maintaining the conduct required of a gentleman, is a tricky balancing act but, due to modern developments, not an insurmountable task.

The smoker in the early stages of withdrawal is not difficult to spot – a look of saintly martyrdom and the sensitive trembling fingers of the poet. These are your target. You are their salvation. Stride confidently forward, smile serenely and announce that help is at hand. Unbeknown to them, you will be carrying a stock of tobacco products as yet unprohibited by the authorities. Proffer a stick of nicotine gum or a nicorette patch to those of a delicate nature or, more robustly, a moist wad of chewing tobacco, or twixt thumb and forefinger, a burgeoning pinch of snuff.

Not all action need be of an overt or confrontational nature. There are subtle pieces of agitprop that can be employed to skilfully manipulate the minds of the populace. One of these is the practice of newspaper doctoring. In the age of the computer, it is a simple matter to turn out bogus newspaper headlines and articles and paste them onto the pages of legitimate daily papers. The finished article may then be left on a seat ready for an unsuspecting member of the public to pick it up. In this way headlines such as, "MOBILE PHONES RESPONSIBLE FOR MALE INFERTILITY, SAY EXPERTS", "EURODISNEY IN NUCLEAR SPILL SCARE" or "READING BAUDELAIRE CURES CANCER" will encourage acceptable modes of civilised behaviour.

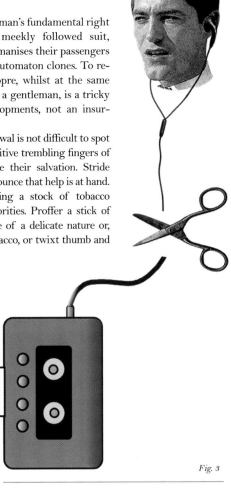

Fig. 3

Tipping

FOR TOO LONG a tyranny has been maintained by a tiny portion of the service industries. Waiters, taxi drivers and hotel porters have been practically the sole recipients of any form of gratuity, with the exception of refuse collectors at Christmas, but their practice is more akin to a form of extortion. Let us question the whole notion of a 'service industry'. It is time for us to tear down the walls of convention that demand us to fish deep into our pockets every time we enter a restaurant, and a crew of waiters, barmen, maître d's and cloakroom attendants gathers around us like a hungry mob, their simpering unctuousness contorting their features into grotesque masks of insincere servility. Compare this with the humble plongeur, who, without the slightest degree of insincerity, calmly loads your dirty dishes into the dishwasher. Do we see him bending over backwards to fulfil your every whim? Does he scrape off the sauce gratin cemented to your plate with an indecent expression of gusto on his face, in the hope of a few extra coins being pressed into his mitt when you depart? Of course he doesn't, because he isn't going to get a tip, no matter how well he does his job. But within the grand scheme of life in a restaurant, is the man who cleans your plate any less important than the man who brings it to your table? A hygienist would probably nominate the dishwasher as the one with the most crucial role in the state of your health. Add to this the implicit dignity of refusing to step on to the first rung of the catering ladder (for within such a vulgar trade, surely it is far more noble to be at the bottom than at the top) and there seems to be every reason to leave a handsome tip for the dishwasher and zilch for the waiter.

Tipping the Deserving is one of the first principles of Chappism, one that can be put into practice by the most inexperienced of our chumrades as they take their first tentative steps on the road towards the Tweed Revolution. Here we list the public service workers whom we believe are most worthy of receiving tips, but let the novice *agent raconteur* use their imagination and tip whenever and wherever they feel the urge.

Bus Conductors

Unlike the heady, jovial days of the Routemaster buses, manned by the willing duo of driver and conductor, the modern system of driver-only buses leaves little opportunity for any rapport between a driver and his flock. A thick pane of glass shielding the driver from the passengers indicates that today's drivers have far more to contend with than the quest for gratuities. However, if you are lucky enough to find yourself on board an old-fashioned Routemaster omnibus, note the way the conductor conducts himself, so to speak. Observe how some conductors, while herding passengers on and off the precarious little platform to the aft of the vehicle, place a paternal arm around the collective shoulders of their flock. Note, too, how some conductors are wont, purely through their own volition and eccentricity, to call out the names of prominent bus stops upon arrival, often with an exaggerated Ealing Comedy intonation: "Haaaanover Squeh, laydeez & gents, thenkin' you!" A coin or two discreetly placed into the conductor's hand should be given in either of these cases. On no account try to include a tip by adding a percentage when paying your fare, as this will draw attention to the transaction and embarrass the conductor.

In the Post Office

Next time you're queuing up in the Post Office, feeling the sap draining out of you every time a robotically cheery voice announces: "Cashier number three, please!" spare a thought for those cashiers themselves. Imagine how their hearts must sink whenever a disabled pensioner for whom English is a third or fourth language comes shuffling up to their counter, and attempts to carry out some complex epistolary task, such as converting her pension into a US$ moneygram and sending it to Paraguay. The Tipster can brighten a Post Office cashier's day twofold; first by purchasing some simple trifle such as a few first-class stamps, secondly by nonchalantly adding, "And have one yourself, my good man/lady." The effect can be further heightened by offering a first-class stamp as a tip when buying second-class stamps.

In Church

The confession box can be a place of great mental stress and spiritual upheaval for any fellow, but imagine what it's like for the priest. Not only must his shoulders bear the weight of so many other people's sins, and his conscience the sordid detritus of the adulterous petit-vulgaroisie, but he also has to sit in a cramped little box for the best part of the day. Reward him for his devotion, but definitely not in kind. "Have one yourself," after receiving a string of Hail Marys is not the way to a priest's heart, for it implies that he, too, is in need of redemption. No, a far more subtle and effective method is to discreetly slip a coin or two under the grate in the confession box. There are those who believe that placing your coin into the donations box near the altar will ultimately reach the priest, on a more spiritual level. This may be true, but he can't very well raid the donations box when he feels like a can of lager, whereas your gratuity will enable him to do this.

American Tourists

Many visitors to the USA have observed that the Americans seem to be continually tipping each other. On this side of the pond, they seem unaware that their habits need adapting to the local culture, and consequently go tip crazy. As a skilled *agent raconteur*, milling about in large towns dressed immaculately, you will probably have many 'greenbacks' pressed into your hand during the tourist season. This may be in return for giving directions to American tourists, or simply for 'making their day' by looking like a quintessential English gentleman. Hang on to those dollar bills, and give them to homeless people begging for money. Being unable to spend them, they will be forced to save them. One day they may even have enough dollars for a visit to the 'Home of the Brave', where they might find better job opportunities than they have found at home.

Teachers

There is no reason to postpone a life of tipping until you reach adulthood. Children as young as seven can begin to enjoy the rewarding life of the Tipster. After a gruelling lesson in painting at primary school, for example, note how the class files out of the classroom, hardly acknowledging the poor woman who has just spent two hours allowing the tiny tots to express their savage, mucky artistic urges all over the room. Show her that you're above this vulgar crowd by slipping a small gratuity into her paint-spattered hand. Your income at this stage in life will not permit anything too ostentatious, but a penny or two will suffice to brighten Miss' day.

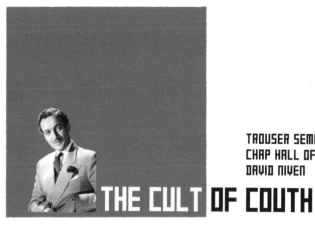

TROUSER SEMAPHORE
CHAP HALL OF FAME
DAVID NIVEN

THE CULT OF COUTH

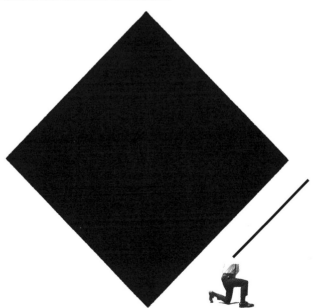

Trouser Semaphore

HAVING GIRDED OURSELVES to enter the arena of pleasantist action, the promulgation of Anarcho-Dandyist principles can only be expected to be achieved if Chaps in the know are able to signal to one another subtly, efficiently and in ways that are completely unfathomable to the questing eyes of the vulgaroisie.

The acquired skill known as Trouser Semaphore enables us to do just that, and is swiftly gaining currency as the only way for people of quality to communicate in an age of rapidly escalating background noise levels. Typically, at the race track or at unexpectedly

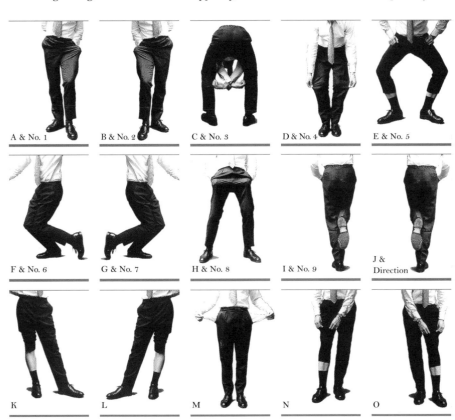

A & No. 1 B & No. 2 C & No. 3 D & No. 4 E & No. 5

F & No. 6 G & No. 7 H & No. 8 I & No. 9 J & Direction

K L M N O

rumbustious parties, attempts to make oneself heard above the general hubbub can prove exasperating and, as often as not, utterly futile. Within the space of a week, and with minimal amount of application, it is possible to gain skills of incalculable worth. Across the floor of a crowded cocktail gathering, you too will be able to convey your innermost thoughts, revolutionary sentiments and deepest needs to like-minded individuals, using nothing more than the flexibility of one's physique and the rough pliability of one's trouser cloth. Surely, there is no sight more moving than a man and three square yards of carefully-tailored cavalry twill moving in perfect harmony.

A note of warning, however: practicing Trouser Semaphore does require a certain level of physical alacrity and suppleness of movement, and is therefore not recommended for extended periods of use by older or incapacitated Chaps who may be suffering from lumbago, arthritis or the physical inertia often associated with excessive port consumption.

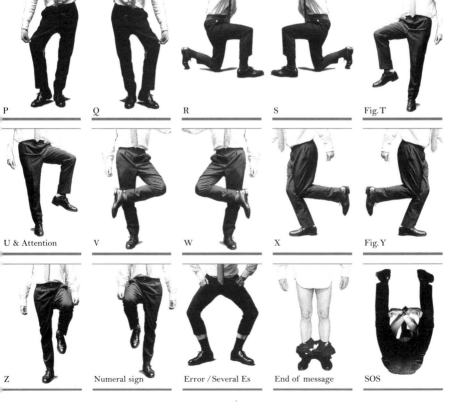

P

Q

R

S

Fig. T

U & Attention

V

W

X

Fig. Y

Z

Numeral sign

Error / Several Es

End of message

SOS

Ad Captandum Vulgus

THERE ARE CERTAIN HISTORICAL PERSONAGES who were active in furthering the causes of Chappism when it was still considered too radical a movement to openly ally oneself with. Those were the dark days of McCartneyism, when long-hairs and drug-addicted rock musicians persecuted those in possession of elegant clothes or trim moustaches. The Committee for the Investigation of Unbeatnik Activities drew up an extensive list, known as the 'Uncool List', of high-profile actors, musicians and artists. Anybody who enjoyed wearing well-pressed trousers, smoking a pipe and drinking Earl Grey tea, instead of snorting marijuana and fouling their flared trousers, was added to the list.

McCartneyism spread like a nasty virus throughout every branch of the arts, and it is fair to say that these industries suffered as a result. Among those on the 'Uncool List' during the 60s were David Niven, Terry-Thomas, James Mason, Leslie Phillips, Peter O'Toole, Rex Harrison, Charlie Watts and Gilbert & George.

The CAD maintains a policy of decorating certain outstanding characters whose unswerving dedication to Chappism did much to further our cause. Thus, all of the above will receive an honorary FBE (Fellow of the British Empire), some of them posthumously. In one outstanding case, we have decided to award one of these first-class fellows with an honorary knighthood. For his lifetime dedication to the tenets, beliefs and causes of Chappism, David Niven is made a Knight of the Realm of the Sock-Suspender.

THE QUEST FOR
David Niven

IF A SINGLE 20TH century figure could be said to embody the spirit of Chappism, then such a fellow would have to be handsome, suave, sophisticated, urbane, elegant, charming, witty, an excellent raconteur and bon vivant, and he would have carried himself through the highs and lows of his life with dignity, panache and savoir-faire. He would also need to be the owner of a first-class wardrobe and a splendid pencil moustache. It soon becomes clear that the only real candidate is the actor David Niven.

One of David Niven's best-known film roles was Phileas Fogg in *Around the World in 80 Days*, filmed during 1955–6 by Michael Anderson. The film charts the adventures of Jules Verne's reserved Englishman, in his attempt to win a circumnavigatory wager made with his companions at the Reform Club. We dispatched a special Chap correspondent, Sholto Douglas, to follow the film crew to its various global locations while the movie was being made, with instructions to award Mr Niven with an honorary CAD Knighthood for his services to the cause of Chappism. Here is Sholto Douglas' report of his quest for David Niven. . .

Suez, 19th March 1955

My first port of call is Suez in Egypt, where various quayside scenes are being filmed. The port is bustling with its usual gaggle of seamen, traders, *fellahs* and porters, and Michael Anderson's film crew can be spotted here and there, but Niven is nowhere to be seen. Having consulted my copy of Jules Verne's novel, I read that Phileas Fogg tries to get his passport stamped at the British consul's office.

My enquiries reveal that Mr Niven has indeed been filmed in the consul's office, but several hours ago. He then boarded a private jet bound for Bombay, to film his next scene.

Bombay, 20th March 1955

With great difficulty and expense, I manage to secure a passage to India on an RAF aircraft headed for Bombay. I while away the journey in the windowless hold by reading the first volume of David Niven's autobiography, *The Moon's a Balloon*, where I learn of his military career before becoming an actor.

Born on 1st March, 1910 to a Scottish father and a French mother, David Niven attended Stowe public school before gaining a place at Sandhurst. His 18 months of army training went swimmingly until he filled in his War Office form, in which cadets name their three choices of regiment for commission. Niven's first choice was the Argyll and Sutherland Highlanders. With characteristic devil-may-care, the 18-year-old cadet wrote as his third choice 'anything but the Highland Light Infantry', then one of the least prestigious of all the Highland regiments. Someone at the War Office returned Niven's little joke by swiftly commissioning him into the Highland Light Infantry.

Niven began his commission as an officer in Malta, where he befriended the eccentric Trubshawe, who never went anywhere without a briefcase containing whisky bottle, soda siphon and two glasses. The single piece of active military service that Niven's battalion saw in Malta occurred when some Maltese drunkards threw some stones at the barracks. A single charge with bayonet by a lone private dispelled them, and Niven settled down to four more years of regimental duty entirely untroubled by anything as vulgar as military action.

Niven learnt during his years in the Highland Light Infantry that he secretly harboured no real desire to gain military rank, and that he was far more ambitious when it came to getting on the lists of Mayfair society hostesses while on shore leave in London. There he met a pretty American deb named Barbara Hutton, who invited the dashing young Niven to spend Christmas at her family's home in New York. Prohibition was raging throughout America, but Niven's charm and savoir-faire soon established him with the rich New York set, for whom bottles of bourbon seemed to magically appear wherever they went. This three-week glimpse of Bacchanalian splendour dispelled what little was left of the 22-year-old Niven's military ambition. When he returned to England, he wrote his letter of resignation from the Highland Light Infantry on Club stationery in Whites of Piccadilly.

Bombay, 21st March 1955

Upon arrival in Bombay, I immediately consult Verne for advice. I read that while Phileas Fogg's eager French manservant, Passepartout, went and got into all sorts of trouble in a Hindu temple, Fogg himself was content to dine at the station before proceeding with his journey. While wholly supportive of this peculiarly English style of tourism, I realise with dismay that, once again, I will not encounter Niven here, for his character does not feature in a single incident taking place in Bombay. I am beginning to feel much like the detective character Mr Fix, played by Robert Newton in the film, who follows Phileas Fogg on his circumnavigation in the mistaken belief that he must be arrested for a robbery. Whenever Fix arrives at each of Fogg's destinations, his quarry seems to have just departed. Perhaps, just as Fix approaches Passepartout to get information on his master, I must speak to Cantinflas, the Mexican actor playing Passepartout, if I am to get closer to Niven.

There are many Hindu temples in Bombay, and after scouting around several of them, I find one with a film crew clustered around it. Leaning against a wall is a swarthy, handsome fellow dressed as a 19th century valet. Cantinflas, undoubtedly.

"Hello there, aren't you the fellow starring with David Niven in *Around the World in 80 Days?*"

He looks rather confused. "Niven, yes. 80 Days, yes."

"Do you happen to know where I can find Mr Niven?"

"Mr Niven he sleeping."

Aha. "And which hotel, pray, would he be sleeping in?"

Cantinflas taps his nose to suggest a well-kept secret. How infuriatingly like Passepartout is this fellow's loyalty to his 'master'! I am about to offer him some money in exchange for the hotel's name when I remember that, though not skilled in the English language, Cantinflas happens to be one of Mexico's best-loved and highly paid actors.

I now realise that the only way to prevent continually lagging behind Niven is to arrive at his next destination before he does. Another consultation of Verne teaches me that, at the close of an incident involving an elephant, a suttee and a charming young lady (played by Shirley MacLaine), the action moves to the Far East, beginning with Hong Kong. The flight to Hong Kong from Bombay is roughly the same distance as the one from Suez, and makes another huge dent in my Chap expense account, but my determination is strong. I am on a civilian aircraft this time, and I devote most of the journey to *The Moon's a Balloon*. I learn of Niven's extraordinary entry into a Hollywood film career.

After resigning from the Highland Light Infantry, Niven returned to the US, where he drifted in and out of various jobs – cocktail waiter, bootlegger, pony racer – before trying his hand at acting. Arriving in Hollywood in 1934, Niven was just another rookie in search of stardom. The agency he registered with already had plenty of British actors on its books, but Niven's advantage over them was his string of society contacts. The wealthy young ladies of his acquaintance clearly saw the polished man of style beneath the down-at-heel film extra, whose accommodation consisted of a cupboard wedged between the lift shaft and the air conditioning unit at a modest hotel. One such lady friend invited him for a weekend at Montecito. Niven packed his frayed dinner jacket and thumbed a ride up US Highway 101, arriving in Montecito in a fruit truck in plenty of time for dinner.

The weekend was centred on a huge party aboard HMS Norfolk, riding at anchor nearby at Santa Barbara. Niven bumped into a pal from his army days, Anthony Pleydell-Bouverie. The festivities raged far into the night; Niven missed his Montecito hostess's departure, and was offered a bunk for the night on board the ship. When he awoke, the following morning, HMS Norfolk was gathering speed into the Pacific Ocean. Dishevelled, hungover and with his dinner jacket looking even more frightful, Niven went in search of the Captain. He describes the scene with characteristic style in The Moon's a Balloon:

"In the Captain's dining room, the Admiral was waiting, a spare, ruddy, typical sailor.

'Morning, Niven.'

'Morning, sir.'

'Enjoy yourself last night?'

'Very much thank you, sir.'

'Care for a pink gin?'

'Thank you, sir.'

There I stood in my dinner jacket, wondering, and there, half an hour later, I sat having luncheon, still wondering. Small talk, shop talk, Malta talk, Bermuda talk, but the subject of my presence never broached."

After luncheon, a solution was found for the involuntary stowaway. HMS Bounty, an 18th century vessel recreated for the filming of Mutiny on the Bounty, was sailing close by as a publicity stunt. The Captain of HMS Norfolk utilised some ancient clause of maritime law to persuade the captain of HMS Bounty to take Niven back to shore. The unknown British actor was lowered onto a waiting dinghy and rowed to HMS Bounty, in the company of Frank Lloyd, the film's director, and Robert Montgomery, then a leading Hollywood actor.

Once on dry land, Niven was introduced to Edmund Goulding, another Hollywood bigwig, who was so impressed by the story of Niven's arrival that he offered him a screen test. He insisted that Niven do the test in the same scruffy 'tuxedo' that he had now been wearing for over 24 hours. The screen test, according to Goulding was 'lousy', but it opened a door into Hollywood that had previously been firmly shut. Niven was given a non-speaking part in Mutiny on the Bounty, and it was only another year before he played the lead in Thank You, Jeeves.

Thus began a long career in Hollywood, with early successes including The Charge of the Light Brigade, Dinner at the Ritz and The Prisoner of Zenda. The last film Niven made during this formative period was Raffles, which he only just finished before war broke out in Europe.

Hong Kong, 22nd March 1955

Upon arrival in Hong Kong, I head for the best hotel on the island, the Peninsula. An informative receptionist saves me the bother of checking in. She meets my enquiries about film crews and whatnot with the intelligence that Mr Anderson's crew will not be coming to Hong

Kong at all, despite many scenes taking place here. She read in a film magazine that all the Hong Kong scenes are to be filmed in Shanghai, the next port of call in both book and film. I had not anticipated a demonstration of China's inter-urban railway system, but at least I have plenty of reading to do on the 21-hour journey. Dipping into Verne once again, I am struck by the extraordinary similarity between David Niven's nautical entry into Hollywood, and a spectacular scene in *Around the World in 80 Days* set in Shanghai. Phileas Fogg and his party are on a private schooner bound for Shanghai, where they must catch a steamer to Yokohama, Japan. Only three miles from Shanghai, running late due to bad weather, they see the Yokohama-bound steamer leaving port. Fogg's entire fortune depends on his catching that ship, so he fires a distress signal from the schooner and flies the flag at half mast. The steamer, obeying an ancient clause of maritime law, comes to their rescue.

Shanghai, 23rd March 1955

Having devoured Verne during my rail journey, I have familiarised myself with all the key scenes involving Phileas Fogg set in both Hong Kong and Shanghai. The principal of these takes place on Hong Kong harbour, when Mr Fix informs Fogg that the steamer for Yokohama has left without him. During my 21-hour rail journey, I had not neglected my Niven, catching up with the development of his Hollywood career.

During the filming of Raffles, *Niven befriended the screenwriter, then a little-known author named F Scott Fitzgerald. The friendship came about mainly because Niven let the writer keep his daily crateful of Coca-Cola in his fridge. This was the only drink Fitzgerald was allowed on set, and Niven also let him sleep off frequent hangovers on the bed in his trailer. When the news arrived of Hitler's invasion of Poland, Niven announced, with renewed patriotic zeal, his intention of signing up. British subjects were not yet being conscripted, but he got around this by asking a relative to send a false telegram to persuade his studio bosses that his country needed him. He fulfilled his contract by completing work on* Raffles, *which Fitzgerald had then been dropped from as a writer. The last that Niven saw of his Coca-Cola-swigging chum was when they were filming a cricket scene in a field in Pasadena. Suddenly Fitzgerald emerged from some bushes, and began weaving drunkenly across the ersatz cricket field towards Niven, yelling, "Hey buddy! Where the helluvya been, buddy?" He was led to the actor's dressing room while filming was finished, and later dragged Niven to a local bar to "drink all the rum in California." A year later, at the height of the Blitz, Niven read in the newspaper of F Scott Fitzgerald's death from tuberculosis.*

Niven found more enthusiasm for the Army now there was a real war to fight. He first became a Major in the elite Phantom Squadron, then a Lieutenant Colonel in the Commandoes, playing an active part in the Normandy landings of 1944.

Niven was welcomed back to Hollywood as a battle-scarred hero, and the film roles came in thick and fast, the most notable being Powell/Pressburger's A Matter of Life and Death. *His next prominent role was the one he is filming now, in 1955, and if only I knew more about it, I might be able to catch up with Mr Niven to give him his CAD knighthood.*

Shanghai, 24th March 1955

It is with pure joy that I arrive at Shanghai harbour. Not only is the quayside busy with film extras, key grips and cameramen, but the scene being filmed involves Niven himself. Peering into the centre of the crowd, I alight on Niven's handsome visage, which shines like a beacon from among the other actors and the extras in the scene. The blue-grey eyes twinkle beneath generous eyebrows, the lips quiver good-humouredly under an impeccable pencil moustache, the hair gleams in a dashing wave above the forehead. His carriage is assured and confident, yet he turns his attention to anybody who speaks to him with an air of personable attentiveness and charm – in short, a gentleman on all counts.

Once the scene is finished, everybody disperses and the crew begin to gather up their equipment. Mr Niven is about to depart with Miss MacLaine and Mr Newton, but changes his mind, and begins to walk in the opposite direction, completely alone! This is my chance!

"Mr Niven, Mr Niven! I wonder if I might have a quick word?"

"Why certainly. What can I do for you?" Niven turns to me with rapt attention. The epitome of civility, even to a complete stranger.

Once I explain to him the purpose of my visit, and briefly outline the difficulties I have had in locating him, he manages to both laugh and show sympathy at the same time. "Dear me! I *am* sorry. If you'd only cabled me in advance, you could have given me the award in Suez. Well, never mind. Now that you've found me, what happens next?"

I can hardly believe by ears. David Niven's movements are to be dictated by me, a humble Chap correspondent!

"The ceremony is brief," I assure him, "all we need is a quiet room and about ten minutes."

"Then I suggest we repair to my hotel."

THE DETAILS OF CHAP KNIGHTHOODS are shrouded in secrecy – suffice to say that a ritual involving a cut-throat razor, a briar pipe and a length of scarlet velvet was performed in Mr Niven's hotel room. He emerged from the ceremony with the title of David Niven, Knight of the Realm of the Sock Suspender, *Ad Captandum Vulgus*, 1955.

A DELICIOUS
STRAIGHTJACKET

REVOLUTIONARY ETIQUETTE
LAVATORIAL ETIQUETTE
CASE STUDY NO. 1
COUNTER-VULGARITY

Revolutionary Etiquette
in Close-up

'**GOD IS IN THE DETAIL**,' if we are to believe the utterances of Mies van de Rohe, and despite this minimalist architect's wrong-headed hostility towards dainty cornices, pediments and gothic finials, on this particular matter he might just have a point. It is in the minutiae of a gent's actions and his fastidious attention to daily niceties that true divinity lies.

Vast tomes have been dedicated to the intricacies of manners and courtliness, and whilst the general remit of this volume is to proffer a code of etiquette in general, here for a few brief pages we are able to concentrate on the fine tuning that will mark the Anarcho-Dandy as a force to be reckoned with.

The dawn of the Tweed Revolution and the resultant era of neo-foppism, once accomplished, will require a rewriting of all existing codes of gentlemanly behaviour.

Traditionally, etiquette has existed for two specific reasons. Firstly, to make one's interchanges with one's fellow man pleasant, bearable and civilised. And secondly, to assist a ruling class to assert its superiority over the common man and enforce uniformity of behaviour. While The Chap is happy to endorse the former, the latter should be regarded as hopelessly outmoded and despicably retrograde. Today's Anarcho-Dandy may favour savagely-refined tailoring, use common courtesy as his modus operandi and worship at the door of arthouse cinema and avant-garde pipe smoking techniques, but he can *never* be accused of being a snob.

In the new age, all shall have the right to carry lavender-scented hankies and lounge for hours on end on Persian divans imbibing vast quantities of laudanum from a Bedouin girl's navel. Surely this is the natural order of things.

Whilst etiquette once excluded or enslaved vast tracts of humanity, now it must be constructed to set us free. This is easier said than done. Old habits die hard. A vulgar elite (the grand-vulgaroisie) that includes popstars, lottery winners, After-Eight-wielding captains of industry and self-righteous media moguls, will not give up without a fight. They will use their garbled and half-baked notions of etiquette as a weapon to repel all pretenders to their nouveau riche domain. Over the following pages you'll find a plethora of suggestions on how to employ a revolutionary approach to negotiating polite society.

Meeting and Greeting

On the face of it nothing could be simpler. An ardent, "How d'you do" answered with an equally forthright, "How d'you do" might seem the sum total of worldy knowledge when it comes to the art of meeting and greeting. But it should be remembered that the first few seconds of any new acquaintanceship is often all you have in order to project a reasonably accurate impression of who you are and what you stand for. To put it simply, your first six seconds of contact with a fellow human being must announce: "I am a man of reason, a man

A   B

Fig. 1. A. **The Logan** – *A gallant doff, useful for attracting the attentions of young ladies. Note, the aesthetically pleasing L-shape formed by the right arm.*

B. **The Senior Wharton** – *The merest tug of a soft brim produces a restrained and graceful effect on sunny days in the park.*

of culture, a man of stern corsetry and loose morals. The way will sometimes be stony and dark, but with the guiding light of Beelzebub and various slim volumes of decadent poetry I will surely claw my way to the distant chimera of certitude and hope. Come on board and join me on my journey of self discovery." Anything less than this and you have failed.

Any opening, "How d'you do" or, "Very good day to you" should be accompanied by an expert and precise doff of one's headgear. Doffing is sadly a diminishing skill and unfortunately it is not within the scope of this book to do the subject full justice. Interested parties should refer to the seminal study, *The Lost Art of Doffing* by Torquil Arbuthnot and Nathaniel Slipper. Arbuthnot & Slipper identify 74 distinct doffs that cater for various social eventualities and age groups. Here we reproduce two classic stances that are ideal for general everyday usage (Fig. 1).

Immediately follow up any doff with the production of a small box of snuff from one's waistcoat pocket. This should be done with a flourish and the box held for few brief seconds before being passed ceremoniously from the right hand to the left. The prescribed ritual for taking snuff dexterously is one area that a gent should divert from at his peril and one that may take many hours or days to master. Generally, you should rap the box once on its side to centre the contents and then offer it to your acquaintances. On its return, rap the box once more, take a hefty pinch twixt thumb and forefinger, hold it aloft briefly and introduce to the nostrils with precision and no spillage. Inhale sharply without a hint of a sneeze or grimace.

Dealing with Smug Hosts

We may all, once in a while, have been forced to spend a bleak evening at the hands of hosts who turned out to be atrocious snobs hell-bent on social advancement and obsessed with doing things 'correctly'. An Anarcho-Dandy craves freedom through style and any such conformism is liable to raise his hackles and inflate his dander.

The next time you attend such a gathering, don't allow yourself to be intimidated by their little pretensions. They are merely ruses to disguise a soul mired in the infernal torment of paid employment. Their familiarity with the concept of dress-down Fridays will have drawn them to the erroneous conclusion that cocktail parties among friends are events that should be 'informal' yet 'smart'. Philip, taking a few brief hours off from his lucrative job in the City, will be wearing a pair of newly-pressed chinos and a supercilious smile of assured superiority. Hilary, his lovely wife and mother of the twins, will attend in a Little Black Dress and a pair of expensive trainers.

The right tone should be set immediately by announcing one's presence with a calling card. In an age where surplus income is spent on consumer durables such as four-wheel drives, mobile phones, fridge-freezers and villas in Umbria rather than on the expert services of an experienced butler, the practice of delivering one's card might present one with certain practical difficulties. These can be circumvented by employing the services of an unwashed ragamuffin. These are ten-a-penny on the streets of our great conurbations. Hand over a gilt-edged card to a street urchin of your choice and instruct the little fellow, bribed with a few choice coppers from the depths of your trouser pocket, to deliver it to the door of the house where you intend to dine. Scampering up the front steps with alacrity and presenting your credentials to your hosts will actively undermine their overblown opinion of their social standing and put them on the back foot where they firmly belong.

Table Manners

Whether you are attending someone else's or holding your own dinner party, your main objective should be to lead guests away from the usual road of predictable behaviour and tedious conversation, and towards a shared voyage of epicurean delight.

Fig. 2. A refreshingly Dada approach to table setting will permanently lodge your dinner party in the memories of your guests.

In much the same way as caged animals in zoos are kept mentally healthy by being set mealtime tasks by their keepers, dinner guests will find their repast far more satisfying if it is presented as a challenge and an opportunity for self-expression. For example, instead of the dry old formula of a plate flanked by serried ranks of knives, forks and spoons, today's modern host should show a little more ingenuity when selecting eating utensils. The novelty of using a Black & Decker two-speed drill to sheer flakes of the roast beef or a 15-inch spanner to negotiate the foie gras, will firmly place your party in the minds of your guests as a night to remember (Fig.2).

Similarly, when eating food as a guest at a more conventional gathering, stand out from the crowd by utilising cutlery in a pleasingly free-style manner. Use your judgement and intuition to tailor your behaviour to the food being eaten and the company being shared. In some circumstances it is best to abandon the use of eating tools altogether and tackle your food in unarmed combat. This approach is especially suited to meat eaters and vigorous gourmandisers unafraid to attack their food with gusto. Getting the feel as well as the taste of a prime piece of rump steak puts a man in contact with his id and will assure any worried host that their food is greatly appreciated (Fig. 3).

If you are indulging in a *dîner à deux* with a young lady it is permissible to demonstrate your ardour and lubricious intent by eating your food directly from the plate (Fig. 4). Tearing chunks directly from a chicken with your mouth or lapping your soup sensuously from the bowl will leave your lady friend in no doubt as to the depths of your passion.

Fig. 3   Fig. 4

Lavatorial Etiquette

There is one need (a natural and wholesome need) that a gent is compelled to cater to, perhaps several times a day, and which, due to his rarefied sensibilities, he is somewhat reluctant to address publicly, but address it we must. We are talking, of course, of the production and disposal of bodily waste.

As we have already seen in relation to the Shirk Ethic, the lavatory can be a particularly fertile venue for perpetrating a little pleasantist action. But sometimes when a chap is off duty and merely in urgent need of jettisoning his morning cup of lapsang souchong, he will find himself forced to enter the mysterious world of the public lavatory. When a fellow is forced to urinate in the public domain he had better watch his Ps and Qs. Denuding one's nether regions in public is a tricky operation and one that requires dexterity, steady nerves, and discretion. This is, after all, the last place that a gentleman would wish for misunderstandings to occur. Where forthrightness, charm and friendliness might seem admirable traits on the public thoroughfare, such virtues may be misconstrued in the dank subterranean depths of a Victorian pissoir. A fellow should keep himself very much to himself. For reasons that it is not necessary to go into here, it is advisable to avoid the vicinity of young men wearing excessively tight legwear, personal jewellery items or mascara.

Fig. 5

When you first enter the lavatory keep your back upright, walk purposefully and affect a facial expression as neutral and unremarkable as a long weekend in Bournemouth. In the unlikely event that you bump into someone you know, acknowledge them with an abrupt nod, barely perceptible to the naked eye and move swiftly on. Under most circumstances it is far preferable and decorous for a gent to make straight for one of the cubicles therein, but often due to the filthy state of such stalls, the absence of a lock or the presence of drug addicts, this may not be practicable. If you find yourself obliged to micturate in the open, do so with speed and efficiency. Look directly ahead and scrutinise the six square inches of wall ahead of you as if you were admiring a particularly fine passage of brushstrokes in Titian's *Death of Actaeon* in the National Gallery. Throughout the course of your relievement it is sensible to punctuate your progress with a succession of brief coughs to announce to all and sundry that you are happily contained within your own world and do not wish to be disturbed. On completion of your task a brief shake and the merest flex of the knees will signal your departure is imminent. After washing one's hands and checking one's buttons it is time to depart; a tricky task skilfully accomplished.

CASE STUDY:
The Story of Gordon

GORDON WAS A 28-YEAR-OLD chartered accountant when he was spotted by one of our *agents raconteurs*. "I was in a terrible state," he recalls with a winsome smile. "Paid employment had torn away every remnant of my self-esteem and I couldn't see anything beyond career prospects, pension plan and mortgage."

Our operative could tell by his general demeanour of efficiency and briskness, and a countenance clouded by mindless ambition, that he was a soul in torment and in urgent need of assistance.

When Gordon arrived home that evening he discovered a slim Anarcho-Dandyist pamphlet in his suit pocket. After an initial hesitancy, he read avidly, and as he read the scales fell from his eyes. "I realised what a dismal failure my life had been up to that point," he muses. "A job for life, a beautiful wife and two lovely children, membership of the local golf club, health insurance, holidays in Tuscany and a spacious house in a desirable area of the town. God, where had it all gone wrong?"

Today, Gordon bears no trace of the tragic nonentity he once was. He now lives in a cavernous, though somewhat derelict, apartment in one of the more tawdry slum districts of Mexico City. Over the last few years, through numerous liaisons with street girls, he has built up an impressive array of venereal diseases including a few conditions as yet unknown to Western medicine. He is a majestic, if rather theatrical dresser, most of his wardrobe having been acquired through annual clean-outs of the costume department of the city opera house, and his days are spent reclining in drugged reverie on a chaise longue the size of a large family saloon.

His apartment is stripped of all the fripperies of consumerist society, leaving only the bare essentials of civilised living: a few volumes by the likes of Huysmans and de Sade; a well-stocked pipe rack; a kitchen denuded of anything other than a few packets of lapsang souchong and the occasional tub of Gentleman's Relish. In the centre of the room is the rather incongruous spectacle of a Shetland pony tearing chunks of hay from a small bail. "That's Gerrard, my yogi," explains Gordon. "He's able to assume animal form whenever he feels it's necessary. Don't quite know why he does it, but it's tremendously impressive don't you think?"

Gordon is a lucky man, a man to whom Madam Fate has decided to grant the rare accolade of a second chance at the game of life. 🐾

Counter-Vulgarity

COUNTER-VULGARITY IS A QUICK-FIX CURE for those offences against the soul that you are likely to witness on a daily basis. Less aggressive than Random Acts of Common Courtesy, these tactics help chumrades develop their own sense of political integrity through simple demonstrations of the civilised way of doing things. Here are the most common offences committed by the vulgaroisie, and their appropriate ripostes.

Text Messaging

It seems to be a common practice nowadays for people to reach into their pocket or bag during a conversation and pull out their mobile phone. While half-listening to their interlocutor, this miscreant will read any text messages recently arrived on their network, sometimes even composing a reply. This is a piece of distinctly anti-Chappist rudeness, and we suggest the following riposte. In mid-conversation, reach into your jacket pocket and pull out a slim volume of poetry, carefully select a page, and proceed to read a verse or two in complete silence. Then gently place the book back into your pocket and turn to your companion with, "Excuse me. You were saying?" Further exasperate your companion by taking out a little notebook and composing a line or two of verse yourself, heightening the effect by gazing heavenwards and licking the end of your pencil.

 ## Tattoos

Misguided youths have recently discovered a penchant for tattooing unusual parts of their bodies with the traditional markings of ancient cultures such as the Maori. An effective riposte is to give these individuals a tenure in the ancient and traditional institution of the Royal Navy, where tattoos have a potent semiotic relationship to rank, class and military bravura. Once the chumrade has had a nude lady crudely burned into his forearm by a drunken Chinaman in Shanghai, his enthusiasm for this primitive form of decoration will rapidly wane.

Utility Wear

Many people respond to the onset of the winter months not by dusting off their wool overcoats, leather gloves and galoshes, but by parading about the streets dressed as if expecting a blizzard on the north face of K2. The manufacturers of this utility clothing further compound the absurdity by giving themselves names such as Rock & Snow and Khyber Pass. There is only one response to this ludicrous sartorial affectation: crampons. Take these individuals gently by the arm and lead them to the top of a very tall building in the lift. Hand them a set of crampons, a length of rope and a compass, and invite them to climb down a real 'north face'.

Logos

What ruse could the most despotic dictatorship dream up to ensure that all its subjects look the same, than to insist they all wear a designated symbol somewhere about their person? A simple tick, for example, with its connotations of 'right' and 'good'. Wouldn't this be a sinister way of controlling the way those subjects dressed? What if that dictatorship then used the public's enslavement to these symbols to foist propaganda on them, through the medium of celebrity endorsement and cultural events that created an indelible link between the symbol and all things good and enjoyable in life? Wouldn't this lead inexorably to the dictatorship controlling the way its subjects thought?

Incredibly, the majority of young people today wear such universal symbols voluntarily. There is only one suitable riposte. With your nail scissors (see Anarcho-Dandyist Toolkit) carefully cut around the tick logo, adapting the shape into the silhouette of a briar pipe. The results will be twofold: your chumrade will benefit from a beautiful bespoke pipe design on their rucksack and, secondly, said rucksack will soon disintegrate, thus convincing its owner that the producers of both rucksack and logo are not worth purchasing in future. When individual brand loyalty starts to crumble, the brand itself must surely follow.

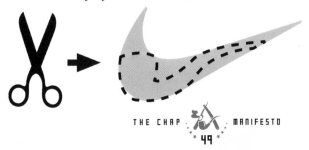

Pavement Diners

What sight could inspire more pity for your chumrades than some poor fellow shovelling noodles into his mouth from a tin-foil container, negotiating the crowds of a busy pavement while buses belch smoke up his trousers? Eating in the street indicates the collapse of table manners and the complete theft of one's dignity by large corporations, who refuse to give workers adequate mealtimes. You may riposte thusly: from a small suitcase, take a folding table and chair, and place them in the path of the roving gourmand. Lay the table with crisp linen, plate, wine glass, cutlery and a vase with a single red rose, and invite the fellow to be seated. Place the contents of his foil container on the plate, and share a bottle of Burgundy and some witty conversation with him.

Gymnasia

Otherwise known as fitness centres, these halls of misery take a perfectly robust individual, perhaps with a bit of surplus fat here and there, and push him on an impossible and uncomfortable journey towards the physique of an athlete. Not only do victims have to suffer the indignity of their perspiration being seen by others, but now they are forced to watch cable television while they pound and grind away on the gymnastic apparatus. The result is that for every pound shed the victim also loses several thousand brain cells. The riposte is simple. Standing at the exit to the gym when its users are departing, read them lines of difficult poetry such as ee cummings. Give them riddles to solve. Show them pictures of abstract paintings. Make them work a bit. After several days of this, they will soon agree with Daniel Defoe that, "The soul is placed in the body like a rough diamond, and must be polished, or the lustre of it will never appear."

Chappism For The Ladies | **wooing**
Smoke Rings

THE
BOUDOIR

OF BROKEN DREAMS

Chappism for the Ladies

THE OPPONENTS OF CHAPPISM, such as beatniks, foreigners and the gainfully employed, have often accused Chappism of being an exclusively male domain. Nothing could be further from the truth. For one, Chappist pursuits, such as writing poetry, making tea, dressing up and smoking, are essentially feminine activities, which allow the male to sprinkle water upon the female orchids blooming within his soul. As for the ladies themselves, their role within the Tweed Revolution can be compared to the Orientals' belief in the balance of yin and yang. Chappism seeks harmony within the polarities of gin (female) and tonic (male). Our devotion to creating a beautiful world comes a close second to our dedication to mixing the perfect G&T. The ladies also make excellent dancing partners and are great fun to be with in the bedroom.

The Role of the Chapette

As stated in *Laying Down The Chamois Gauntlet*, the first principle of the CAD is the radical politicisation of common courtesy. While it is true that Chaps are happy to heap an infinite amount of courtesy and good manners upon the ladies, this does not imply a need to gain the upper hand. Chaps are more than glad to be on the receiving end of such revolutionary acts as hat doffing, giving up seats and smiling. These gestures are crucial signals to fellow *agents raconteurs*, and must be deployed as often as possible, regardless of gender. With regards to home life, Chappism wholeheartedly supports the traditional family unit. However, we do not advocate the assigning of domestic duties such as cleaning, polishing and dusting to the ladies. That's what the servants are for, silly!

Lotions, Potions and Unguents

So, if a lady is to stride into the grand arena of Chappism, where does she begin? In the bathroom, of course, just like the gentlemen. The only difference is that a lady may spend a little less time in there than the Chap. There are also one or two lavatorial procedures peculiar to the ladies, which are the subject of complete mystification to the gentlemen and probably best kept that way.

The philosophy of make-up is far more complex than the philosophy of male grooming, requiring the skill of the artist for the best results. You must aim for the chiaroscuro subtleties of a Caravaggio or a Rembrandt, not the amateurish daubings of a Jackson Pollock. Good lighting is essential: 18 or 20 light bulbs framing the mirror should do the trick, and will remind you to apply your make-up as if you are about to go and receive an Academy Award, rather than to pop down to the shops for a pint of milk.

From Coiffure to Cosmetics

Just as a Chap begins his grooming ritual with a shave, so a lady must first address the sensitive issue of facial hair. The golden rule is: no half measures. Dismiss the Latin affectation of a downy 5 o'clock shadow on the upper lip. Either cultivate the hair into a proper moustache (see *The Semiotics of Hair*) or exterminate it altogether. Upper lip undesirables can be removed by dripping wax from a votive candle above the lip, then ripping it off. To heighten the religious solemnity of this act, feel free to reel off a couple of Our Fathers while the wax hardens. May the Lord protect you from pain, for this method of hair removal does tend to smart a little.

Marlene Dietrich was the pioneer of an 'instant facelift'. This novel technique involves pulling the hair above the ears tightly to the back of the head and fastening it with hairpins, giving the skin around the eyes a youthful tautness for a few hours. Don't forget to re-tighten every so often during the evening or your companions will think you are the victim of some strange wasting disease.

Contrary to the belief maintained by blonde television personalities with learning difficulties, the blend of sunbed-orange skin and peroxide-blonde hair is not the slightest bit appealing to gentlemen. The most desirable complexion is a healthy, lightly aroused glow, with a hint of malice around the cheekbones. A sensual shade of pink can be achieved by buffing the cheeks with a scrubbing brush between bathing and applying make-up. Also, try to avoid anything likely to give you coarse skin, such as sunlight, office work or celibacy.

The one effect ladies should avoid when applying make-up is the so-called natural look, which is a chronic waste of time, money and whale blubber. Figure 1 shows the make-up equivalent of a painstakingly constructed piece of dull minimalist sculpture, while Figure 2 has all the attributes of a Renaissance fresco in the cupola of a Florentine chapel.

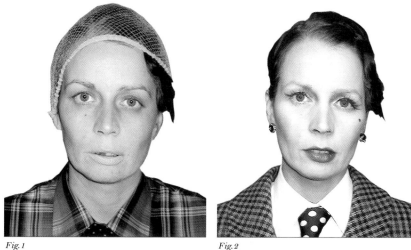

Fig. 1   *Fig. 2*

Make-up: the Finer Points

Eyebrows

To achieve the haughtiest effects they must be shaved off and replaced with false eyebrows made from mouse skin. Ask your pet shop for the darkest mice they have, and before alarm bells start ringing, don't worry. If mouse skin is removed carefully, it does grow back, so you won't have to buy a new mouse every week!

False Eyelashes

Give them two generous coats of black mascara with an applicator made of sea-urchin bristles, not plastic. The result should be thick enough to shade your eyes from sunlight and harsh neon lighting.

Cheeks

A robust, healthy glow can be achieved by vigorously pinching the cheeks between the fingers. A deeper shade of magenta can result from taking frequent nips out of a hip flask, permanently filled with Bloody Mary, kept in the handbag.

Beauty Spot

Offset any underconfident areas with a strategically placed beauty spot. This one diverts attention from the absolute mess this lady has made of her hair.

Teeth

Whiter-than-white they may be post-brushing, pre-first Sobranie of the day, but they will soon gain an unappealing yellow colour. Always carry with you a bottle of hydrogen peroxide and a cotton bud to whiten the chompers.

Facial Hair

Two examples of the suitable treatment of female upper lippery. On the left, a votive candle wax treatment has denuded the upper lip of unwanted infringements. On the right, the hair has been allowed to flourish, creating a pleasing, modern look calculated to win the attentions of more forward-thinking fellows.

Follicular Matters

There is only one road to hirsute mastery, and that is to find the hairstyle that works for you and stick to it until it falls out. Frequent barnet rethinks upset the harmony and stability implicit in the gin nature of the ladies. When it comes to hair colour, it should be treated like poetic inspiration and always come out of a bottle. Here are the four essential Chapette hairstyles and a description of the sort of character you can expect to find underneath them.

A. The Pandora

This is for the lady who has something to hide. The hair frames the face in a protective manner that keeps out strangers and evil thoughts. The Pandora lady only lets in those whom she can really trust. But once you have parted the two sides of this weighty hairstyle, you're in, and you may find it difficult to get out again.

Fig. A

Fig. B

B. The Weimar

This is for the slightly outré lady who frequents cabarets, chain smokes French cigarettes and is possibly attracted to other ladies. A fellow should expect an unconventional approach to the boudoir and a fridge containing nothing except champagne, laudanum and cold cream. This hairstyle looks especially good with a monocle.

C. The Have and Have Not

Ideal for creatures of the night, the HaHN is a resilient, durable hairstyle that can withstand the most punishing social schedule. This lady enjoys casinos, jazz clubs and grand balls in country mansions. She is a good dancer and an expert lover. Men, proceed with caution and expect high levels of romance from this femme fatale.

Fig. C

Fig. D

D. The Belle de Jour

This is for the solid, dependable lady with a fondness for baking, crochet and embroidery. However, there is a feral aspect to her, only revealed once the hair is let down. When she loosens her kirbys and shakes her mane till it fans out around her waist, fasten your seatbelts, gentlemen, it's going to be a bumpy ride.

Coquette of the Walk

Day Wear

A girl in tweed is a lady indeed, so the saying goes in Chapette circles. This tweed two-piece ladies' suit (below) by Bernard Weatherill gives the wearer an elegant insouciance appropriate for day-to-day ambling about the shops or visiting one's turf accountant. It has been combined with a white blouse from Harvie & Hudson of Jermyn Street and a polka-dot silk tie from Budd of Burlington Arcade, brown stockings and brown court shoes by Elliot.

Evening Wear

A lady should never be seen in trousers, not least for stepping out of an evening. This beige two-piece by Huntsman (above), offset by a black feather boa, would make an equally elegant impression at a fashionable restaurant or a Mayfair casino. When lifting the skirt to step out of an aeroplane or over an obstacle, always use a wooden skirt-lifter as opposed to the hand, to avoid marking the hem and corroding the fibres.

"The Road of Accessories . . .

. . . leads to the palace of wisdom," as William Blake would have said, had he been a lady. The full subject of ladies' accessories would be enough to fill several volumes in itself. Here is a tiny selection of the most essential requisites that a Chapette should never leave her rooms without.

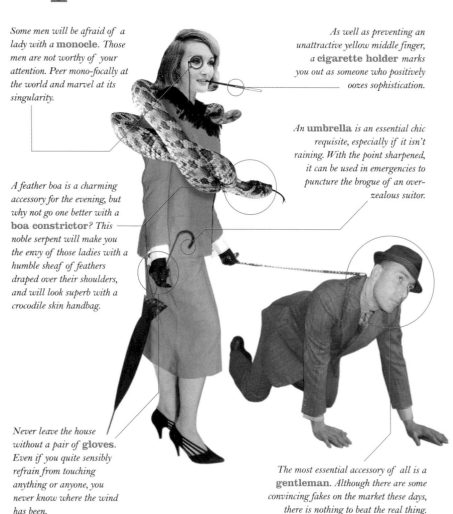

Some men will be afraid of a lady with a **monocle**. Those men are not worthy of your attention. Peer mono-focally at the world and marvel at its singularity.

As well as preventing an unattractive yellow middle finger, a **cigarette holder** marks you out as someone who positively oozes sophistication.

An **umbrella** is an essential chic requisite, especially if it isn't raining. With the point sharpened, it can be used in emergencies to puncture the brogue of an over-zealous suitor.

A feather boa is a charming accessory for the evening, but why not go one better with a **boa constrictor**? This noble serpent will make you the envy of those ladies with a humble sheaf of feathers draped over their shoulders, and will look superb with a crocodile skin handbag.

Never leave the house without a pair of **gloves**. Even if you quite sensibly refrain from touching anything or anyone, you never know where the wind has been.

The most essential accessory of all is a **gentleman**. Although there are some convincing fakes on the market these days, there is nothing to beat the real thing.

The Subtle Art of Wooing the Ladies

AS WE HAVE SEEN, it is not unreasonable for Chaps to meet their female counterparts, the Chapettes. We have also demonstrated a variety of methods of communication, recognisable only to the trained eye, by which a fellow might establish contact with a chumrade of either sex. But what if he's keen to go beyond a mutual exchange of Chappist agit-fop? What if he desires to take the friendship to a higher level? What if his brain ceases to function in any capacity other than to compose romantic poetry and brood in dark rooms, and he begins to lose weight, smoke heavily and affect a listless, abstracted demeanour?

Well, by George, he's going to have to woo the little lady, isn't he!

First Principles

It may sound a tad crude, but wooing a lady is not a million furlongs from betting on a horse. First of all, you must betake yourself to a place where there are lots of ladies. Secondly, you study the size, weight and form of the filly who has taken your fancy, and ask yourself these questions. How does she take to soft ground? What is she like over hurdles? What sort of jockeys have previously had success in her saddle? Thirdly, and most importantly, you look at

the odds. There is little point in betting on the odds-on favourite who will necessitate a huge wager to guarantee a good return. Chaps tend to have more success with rank outsiders, who appreciate their reedy voices and their tweedy ways. Once you have placed your bet, your success is in the capable, though often cruel, hands of providence. Be ready for one of only two outcomes: you are either going to be driven homewards in a hired limousine, quaffing champagne in a romantic arm-lock with your ladylove, or you will be sloping off alone on the 18:36 from Cheltenham to face a quiet depression until the next meet.

Preparation – Grooming

When wooing a lady, be prepared to spend an extra hour or so in front of the glass, on top of your normal grooming procedure. It could mean the difference between losing your shirt and having it removed by silky-smooth manicured hands. Still with cut-throat razor in hand after your shave, deal with any hirsute flashpoints that might horrify a lady. Do your eyebrows meet in the middle? Do your ears look as if furry hermit crabs are trying to escape from them? Do you have chest hair that seems intent on tangling itself around your tie like some sinsiter creeping ivy?

When it comes to bottled scent, Chappist recommendations are quite simple: leave them where they belong on the dressing tables of ageing Latin lotharios. A far more subtle impression can be made by consuming, the previous evening, a handful of rose petals or a sprig of rosemary. Twenty-four hours later, your pores will be seeping a distinct aroma whose top notes your lady friend will find intoxicating.

Locating the Ladies

Where can a fellow expect to find a lady during these so-called enlightened times? A valuable piece of advice is to avoid the places where one used to find ladies aplenty, such as garden centres, nursing homes and supermarkets. These places are now frequented more often by solitary and quite miserable-looking men. Ladies, confusingly, are now to be found in droves in the very places traditionally associated with men: snooker halls, hardware shops and taverns. Take a look at that scruffy, down-at-heel person slouched at the bar in a seedy pub, demanding a seventeenth flagon of ale. Why, it's a lady! Go ahead, make her acquaintance – she'll probably appreciate the company. Try out some of the useful 'Chap-up' lines below on her.

Chat-up Lines ☞ Chap-up Lines

Chat-up Lines	Chap-up Lines
What star sign are you? ☞	Would you care to examine the stars with me? I believe Ursa Minor is looking particularly splendid tonight.
That's a nice dress. Where did you get it? ☞	You must tell me the name of the delightful cloth your dress is made of, so I can have my tailor run me up a cravat from it.
Do you fancy coming to see the Pants at the Forum tomorrow? I've got two tickets. ☞	Please settle an argument between myself and a chum. Was it Schubert or Mahler who composed the Trout Quintet?
You look familiar. Do I know you? ☞	Madam, your profile bears a startling similarity to that of my cousin, the 3rd Duchess of Bedfordshire. Are you perchance related?

Smoke Rings for Wooers

YOUNG LOVERS ARE renowned for their ability to stand motionless in the moonlight, gazing simperingly into each other's eyes for hours on end, saying very little, and occasionally stroking each other's faces. This is the sort of thing ladies love, and to a certain extent a young man is perfectly happy to go along with such nonsense, but it's definitely an activity that can't go on forever. Eventually, after staring vacantly down at one's fingernails, or fidgeting nervously with one's lapels, the only option is to gaze up at the night sky for something better to do. This is the point where a fellow is able to buck up the conversation somewhat by entertaining his ladylove with the fascinating names, tales and statistics pertaining to the planets and constellations. Ladies love this too, but tragically on our urban thoroughfares light pollution from millions of neon street lamps is rendering this particular amorous gambit all but redundant.

The Halo *Once blown allow the smoke ring to hover above one's head for a few brief moments whilst assuming a demeanour of saintly martyrdom.*

The Tube *A witty usage of surfing terminology to describe an elongated smoke ring of gossamer beauty, but with devil-may-care credentials.*

Triple Drift *An elegant effect produced by serial puffing. It requires immaculate timing and a high level of smoke-to-lung breath control.*

So what is a chap to do? Instead of regarding these neon excrescences as an enemy, it is time to harness their incandescence to our own ends. If the lady is unable to see the constellations, then she must be entertained with other phenomena. A dark sky and a bright light provide the perfect conditions for a man of fumatory skills to rivet his amour with a splendid display of advanced smoke ring gymnastics. 🚬

The Great Bear *'Almost indistinguishable from the real thing' Patrick Moore.*

Saturn *A complex and difficult one to master. 'Evocative and sublime' Evening Standard.*

The Love Heart *Always a winner with the ladies. 'Un coeur de théatre' Charles Baudelaire.*

Figure Eight *Deceptively simple configuration requiring surprising agility in the lumbar region.*

Flying Bird *Smoking and origami collide in this original 19th century Zen classic.*

Technical Appendix for Wooers

ONCE YOU HAVE attracted a lady's attention by your singular presence, wit and charisma, it is time to arrange an outing with her. The first outing should be a casual, daytime excursion, which you must use to show the lady all your best qualities. Your aim should be to leave her with an indelible impression of you, so that when she sips her cocoa later in the evening, she is thinking: "My what a splendid fellow! I just cannot seem to get him out of my mind. Can't wait to see him again!" Here are a couple of suggestions for first outings, and how to orchestrate them skilfully.

A Cultural Excursion

While your lady friend will be no stranger to museums and art galleries, try this Chappist slant on such a venture. Make a solo visit to the proposed museum the previous day and study the display information. Ingratiate yourself with the staff by passing the time of day with them and offering them Murray Mints. When you come to visit the museum with your date, you will be a fount of knowledge on the exhibits, and your familiarity with the attendants will give you the air of a man whose life is immersed in culture. Consolidate this at the end of the visit with an unusual request. Rather than inviting her to join you for a cup of coffee (<u>very</u> petit vulgaroisie), inform her at the exit that you will spend another hour alone in the museum, as you feel you have "not studied the ceramics sufficiently."

An Epicurean Excursion

Similar techniques can be applied to a luncheon date. If your date is on a Thursday, visit the restaurant on the previous Thursday, when the same staff will be present. During your solitary meal, frequently call the maitre d' over to request more of their excellent condiments or to compliment the chef on his gravy. Leave an enormous tip, along with your card. When you return the following week with your lady friend, the waiters will not only address you by name, but you will be given the best table in the house, and the lady will be awestruck at the level of attention she receives in your company.

Following Up

There are two distinct approaches to follow-up tactics. Most ladies can be won over with either approach, it is simply a question of which one you can carry off with the most savoir-faire.

1. Complete Indifference

After the first date, disappear off the face of the earth. Then, about 17 years later when the lady is already married with several children, send her a 25,000 word letter in the form of a novel you have published yourself in Bolivia. In the letter, declare your undying love for the lady, which has burned within you like St Elmo's Fire for the last 17 years, even though your tragic disfigurement in a freak boating accident makes a reunion impossible. The lady will then be yours for the taking.

2. Complete Devotion

Immediately after, or even before, your first date with the young lady, appear on her doorstep every morning. Either find a nearby hotel, or sleep in your car if necessary, but make sure that as soon as she leaves the house to go to work, you pop out of the bushes with a brisk, "Good morning!" Don't be put off if she emerges from the house with anybody else, even if it is another fellow. This is probably a ruse to make you jealous. Be courteous but firm. Take her by the arm and stride away, inviting the intruder to make himself scarce, sharpish.

HAIL BACCHUS,
APOTHECARY OF THE INFINITE

GENTLEMANLY AILMENTS
SMOKING IS GOOD FOR YOU
CONSUMPTIVE COSMETICS

Gentlemanly Ailments

OF COURSE THERE IS NOTHING quite so profound as being an invalid (see *Consumptive Cosmetics*, Page 70), and the muse can often be more easily coaxed into one's presence during prolonged periods of illness. Marcel Proust is perhaps the finest example of a man who lost nothing by spending his entire life in a state of ill health. However, the demands of the Tweed Revolution may be hindered if too many of our *agents raconteurs* have taken to their sick beds. So here is an examination of some of the minor ailments that can befall a gentleman, and instructions on how to treat them.

Raconteur's Wrist

Excessive gesticulation during the recounting of an amusing or lewd tale is apt to produce undue strain on the radio-ulnar joint. Frequent bathing of the afflicted wrist in a lukewarm solution of laudanum, champagne and Epsom salts is advised. This treatment is most effective if administered with the patient reclining on a chaise longue while a Moroccan boy glides about the room singing Arabic folk songs.

Cocktail Finger

Though admirably maintained by sophisticated persons when drinking cocktails, the extended finger at the base of a glass can put unpleasant strain on the metacarpals. Allow the weary digit to rest for half an hour or so, during which time you can get one of the servants to administer dry martinis intravenously. Alternatively, occupy yourself in smoking a cigar for an hour or two, though do beware of Smoker's Thumb.

Handshaker's Thumb

This is caused when the hearty greeting of a good pal is expressed through vigorous clasping of his hand. Gentlemen, not known for their tactile qualities, often express all their innermost feelings through hand shaking. Do not, however, feel tempted to shake hands more limply in the hope of resting your thumb. That approach is strictly for the ladies. In short, the cure is to cease shaking hands for a spell. A slight elevation of the hat is perfectly acceptable in polite society, especially if passing on the street.

Brown Study

This can happen to a gentleman at any time, with very little warning. The most common period of occurrence is during prolonged sessions with one's hookah, or while under the influence of opium. The man who has gone into a brown study will suddenly cease all conversation, focusing all his attention upon a crack in the ceiling or on an unusually sombre aspect of his inner mind. Persuade him to occupy himself with a simple toy such as a kaleidoscope. This will bring out his playful side once again, and take his mind of those dark thoughts.

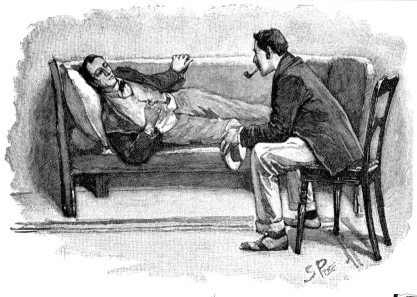

Fox-Trot Fibula

Dancing is all very well as part of an extensive wooing programme, but be careful not to overdo it. Some of today's rhythms can be a little lively, mainly due to the influence of American music. In leading the dance, the male can find himself with a slightly throbbing fibula during a particularly jaunty number. The cure is simple. Cease dancing for a spell, and turn your attentions to wooing your lady through witty conversation and smoking on the verandah.

Housemaid's Knee

The patella can become weakened during prolonged sessions of balancing the housemaid upon your knee while you pretend to be working in the study. A few holes of executive mini-golf should help get the circulation going again, and by all means encourage the housemaid to join in as well, by assigning her the role of executive caddie.

Tailor's Dummy

This can be the result of extensive sessions with your tailor during the fitting of a complicated suit. Out of sheer embarrassment at the close proximity of another man, the whole body goes into a state of rigor mortis. While having the pleasant side effect of making your tailor's job a lot easier, it is advisable to alert him to your condition and request that he leave the room for a few minutes while you compose yourself.

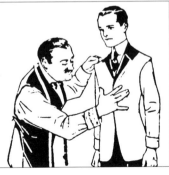

Smoking is Good for You

THE SIMPLE FACT of the matter is that smoking gives you heart disease, increases your chances of stroke and often results in a wide variety of unattractive cancers. But to the chap, idly dallying about his business with head firmly set on the transcendent, these are but a petty price to pay for the camaraderie, exquisite sublimity and downright stylishness that smoking affords. A fellow instinctively knows that without smoking's attendant dangers, what amounts to his religion, his philosophy of life, indeed his *raison d'être*, would be so much trickling water under the bridge of eternity. No man, be he lowly costermonger or Hollywood idol, ever received praise for the consumption of bran, vegetable matter or vitamin tablets. Indeed, it would be impossible to consume such comestibles stylishly even if one tried. But smoking – that's a different matter.

Tobacco smoke contains precisely zero calorific content and yet is as satisfying and enticing as any three-course meal. Smoking taints your breath and yellows your teeth and yet at the same time makes you utterly irresistible to the ladies. Smoking ultimately destroys you but at the same time makes you a prince among men.

As injurious as tobacco products may be physically, their psychological, transcendental and social benefits are nigh on impossible to beat. Figure 1, for example, illustrates the psychochemical interface between a jaunty fellow's stylish cranium and his eagerly receptive lungs. Freshly intoxicated by a dangerously heady cocktail of nicotine, tar and synthetic chemicals, the bloodstream almost

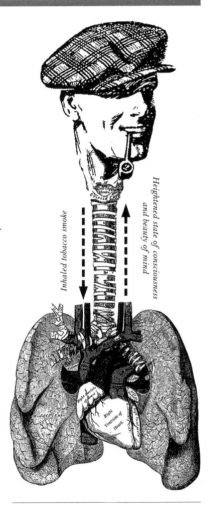

Inhaled tobacco smoke

Heightened state of consciousness and beauty of mind

Fig.1. Demonstrating the benefits that may be achieved via the psychochemical interface.

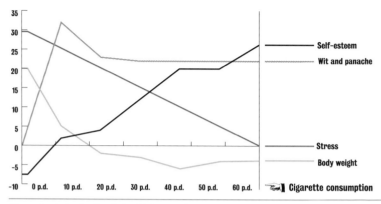

Fig. 2. Graph showing the relationship between cigarette consumption per day (p.d.) and the percentage reduction or gain in levels of stress, wit and panache, body weight and self-esteem.

instantaneously delivers a kick start to the tired and jaded brain, rendering it susceptible to reverie, profundity and nuance. In short: poetry is born.

Some of the last century's finest scientific, political and artistic achievements were conceived of through the timely intervention of smoking. Does anyone seriously contest that Churchill's browbeating of Hitler was anything other than a triumph of nicotine usage over abstemiousness? We think not. Would any scholar of literature deny the pivotal role of tobacco in the production of such classics as *Fear and Loathing in Las Vegas*, *The Old Man and the Sea* and *Northanger Abbey*. Hardly. It is an eminently deniable yet highly credible conjecture that Martin Luther King, Mother Teresa, Watson and Crick, Albert Einstein, Aristotle, Pablo Picasso, Leonardo di Vinci, Victor Hugo, Kate Winslet and Lassie the Wonder Dog all, at one time or another, had habits that amounted to over 60 cigarettes a day.

It is in a social context, however, that smoking really comes into its own. Carefully perusing Figure 2 we may readily conclude that apart from its pronounced life-threatening qualities, smoking is very good for you indeed. With a modest indulgence of 10 cigarettes a day, just watch your wit, general panache and self-esteem soar on a spiralling trajectory to unprecedented heights, and simultaneously feel stress, everyday cares and body weight fall away, leaving you shimmering with beauty and tremendous fun to be with.

As your addiction grows, sit back and cheerfully puff away in the sure knowledge that whatever is happening to your lungs, your popularity and social standing are in the rudest of rude good health.

If you need to be convinced, we have recourse to science as our guiding light. In recent laboratory trials funded by the CAD, maverick man of science, Professor Compton Pauncefoot took a random sample of 60 male rats. Twenty of these rats were reared solely on a diet of dry martinis, canapés and lung-searing Turkish cigarettes. A second group of 20 received the martinis and canapés but no cigarettes. And the final 'control' group of 20 had their cigarette ration replaced by a placebo cigarette containing no nicotine.

After 10 weeks, 20 mature female rats were introduced into the enclosure. Nature, robustly taking her course, led within a six-week period to the birth of 108 offspring. Subsequent research into the genetic make-up of the offspring to ascertain the parentage of each kitten, gave the the following result.

Of the 108 kittens: 18 turned out to be the progeny of the non-smoking rats and 27 were produced by fathers who smoked placebo cigarettes. But a resounding 63 were discovered to contain the genetic make-up of the smoking rodents who throughout the course of the experiment had been observed lounging rather louchely in the corners of the cage feigning indifference to their female quarry. Conclusive proof, if proof be needed, that smoking even in the shabby, ordure-strewn world of the rat, is one of the mightiest aphrodisiacs known to science.

We clearly don't need to anthropomorphise to prove our point, but merely to observe and to act. Striding along the public thoroughfare, the casual observer may often mark those small throngs that huddle outside offices, in all weather, in the name of tobacco. These bands of sturdy individualists gathered together in the face of persecution and hostile, draconian law that denies a man his fundamental right to smoke, speak eloquently of the camaraderie, solidarity and saintly martyrdom of an oppressed people.

For years now, a nonchalantly-held cigarette has been synonymous with the timeless concept of 'style'. What would Rita Hayworth, Humphrey Bogart, Ingrid Bergman, Betty Davis and a whole legion of movie stars be without the aid of the humble cancer-stick? The CAD, as men of vigour, men of flesh and blood, men of rich emotional life can answer this question unequivocally: "Nothing, nothing at all."

So we earnestly exhort you to tear up your health insurance plan, renege on your fitness club membership and pay up front for your funeral, and invest in the most stylish tortoise-shell cigarette holder that money can buy.

Consumptive Cosmetics

Good morning Muse, what's wrong?
Something you saw last night is left in your hollow eyes;
Your colour's bad, your cheeks are cold
With horror, with madness! – and you don't say a word.

The Sick Muse
CHARLES BAUDELAIRE

WE CAN ALWAYS RELY ON good old Charles Baudelaire to articulate a sentiment so subtle, so complex, so recherché, that the vulgaroisie would not recognise it if it walked up and boxed their ears. And is it any wonder that the muse was as prey to sickness as the poet himself when you consider the lifestyle Baudelaire led? By the age of 40, a combination of syphilis, strokes and hard living had reduced him to a physical and mental wreck, on the verge of insanity and paralysis.

Had Baudelaire been the picture of health, with ruddy cheeks, a robust frame and hearty manner, it is doubtful whether he would have been taken very seriously as a poet. In the 19th century, the fashionable look among bohemians was the wan and sickly pallor of the tubercular poet. "When I was young, I could not have accepted as a lyrical poet anyone weighing more than 99 pounds," Théophile Gautier tells us. A celebrated femme fatale of the period, Princess Belgiojoso, strolled along the boulevards of Paris as gaunt and pale as death in person. But this was not the result of bulimia or a steady diet of Evian water, cocaine and lettuce leaves such as today's ladies of fashion maintain. Tuberculosis produced 'the look' without any effort at all on the patient's part. The disease's victims were many, though it seemed to favour sensitive, artistic temperaments. "TB was thought to etherealize the personality, expand the consciousness, to aestheticize death," according to Susan Sontag. "The TB sufferer was a dropout, a wanderer in endless search of the healthy place."

With TB being very difficult to catch these days, and relatively easy to cure, how can we cultivate the wasted demeanour of the consumptive, and thus impress upon our friends the sensitive, aesthetic nature of our souls? The answer lies in cosmetics. Gentlemen, prepare to rummage through a lady's handbag or, better still, her bathroom cabinet. Ladies, prepare to make yet another visit to the chemist with a gentleman's funds (the very mention of the words 'ladies' requisites' will have him shielding his eyes while handing you wads of fivers).

The most important aspect of a consumptive's demeanour is the face. Start with an all-over layer of foundation of the palest shade you can find, to which you have added a touch of green to emphasise the sickliness. A delightfully feverish sheen can be added by daubing Vaseline on the forehead and cheekbones. Now to the eyes. Use an eyebrow pencil to draw rings around them, rubbing the black until it blends smoothly with the pale foundation. Some dark mascara, with a touch of Vaseline, will give the eyelids a deathly hue. To the lips, apply a hint of blue, suggestive of a man about to breathe his last. The tongue should appear dull, matt and coated. A black coating can be achieved by regular consumption of red wine, producing a nice dark contrast to the pallid visage (Fig. 1).

Excessive smoking should encourage a hacking cough. Increase the strength of your brand to help this or, better still, smoke cheroots and inhale them. It is all the more effective when you cough if the whole body rattles, an effect easily created with practice.

Spend all your waking and sleeping hours clad in pyjamas and dressing gown. Throw all your other clothes away so you won't be tempted to get dressed. Make sure visitors call in the middle of the afternoon, to emphasise that you are completely inactive. Always receive visitors in bed, under an exaggerated amount of bedclothes. A few additions to your room can encourage the heady aroma of the invalid's bedchamber. Leave the tops off bottles of medicine, allowing their clinical odours to seep into the room. Used bandages, swabs and cotton wool can be left in sinister mounds near the bed, allowing your friends to conjecture the worst.

Your social niceties will need radically rethinking. Be vague about remembering people's names, and pretend to have forgotten they were coming to see you. Act as if every meeting could easily be your last – make melodramatic gestures and grand statements. Languish on a huge pile of pillows, one arm tragically outstretched, while you quote the stanzas of Coleridge and Keats that you would like to have read at your funeral. Generally try to give the impression that, unlike ordinary people, you are in a heightened state of lyrical sensitivity, inhabiting an ethereal plane of existence which straddles life and death. Emphasise this by allowing some of your sentences to trail off. . . Pretend to fall asleep when being told a fascinating tale. When your friends try to rouse you, stare at them uncomprehendingly for a minute, as if you were looking into the eyes of God or the Devil.

Before

After

Fig. 1. Examples
showing how cosmetics
can create the elegant
demeanour of the consumptive.

WORK WILL BLIGHT YOUR EXISTENCE

DEALING WITH THE MINISTRY OF UNEMPLOYMENT

THE SHIAH ETHIC

CASE STUDY NO. 2

SPANKING MAMMON

The Shirk Ethic
Entering the World of Work

SURELY THERE IS no activity more calculated to corrode the human spirit than paid employment. A right-thinking fellow will usually do all that is within his powers of ingenuity to avoid it, but there comes a time in every man's life when (due to pressing gambling debts or the need to fund a mounting barbiturate addiction) he will be obliged to bite the bullet and enter into the unfamiliar world of work.

Paradoxically, in some ways the best sort of part-time job for a Chap to acquire is mindless, repetitive employment in a factory, wholesale warehouse or local government unit. Despite the demeaning nature of such work, keeping one's grey cells completely detached from the task in hand will ensure that they remain as pristine and unsullied as delicate snowdrops flowering in harsh winter climes, and will provide them with ample time for musing and reverie. Rubbing shoulders with the simple working man and partaking of his rough-hewn wisdom is far more rewarding than spending long hours in the company of thrusting young executives who, generally speaking, have no redeeming qualities at all. At the same time, you will be left in no doubt that this period of employment is a temporary measure and something that must come to an end as soon as is humanly possible.

Realistically speaking though, due to a foppish and enervated countenance, the chances are that you will end up working in some form of office environment. You will soon discover that offices are almost identical to factories except they are centrally heated, usually carpeted and their products are a good deal less useful. Offices have the distinct advantage of providing fiscal recompense somewhat greater than the minimum wage, which in turn reduces the period of hard labour that you are obliged to endure. But beware, many pitfalls await the unsuspecting. The modern business employs various tactics to break down the spirit of its employees. These include the offer of permanent positions, promotions and bonuses, and sending their staff on 'motivational weekends' in order to brainwash them into thinking that what they are doing is 'team-orientated' and 'worthwhile'. A high level of concentration must be maintained at all times to avoid being corrupted by such frippery. As long as you keep your wits about you, you will soon realise that the world of work simply involves shuffling the world's matter about from A to B and back again, at somebody else's behest and for somebody else's benefit. This 'matter' may take the form of pieces of paper, electrical pulses on a computer screen, currency, metal ores or foodstuffs, but essentially the idea is always the same.

Sidling into the office for the first time, after having risen at God-knows-what unsavoury hour, you will gain the general impression that you have reached the lower depths of hell. Indeed you have. You will be greeted by a cavernous room filled with blonde-wood desks, computer monitors, ringing telephones and the alarming hubbub of industrious personnel. This is where amour propre is sacrificed on the altar of profit and commerce. This is where back stabbing and ambition run roughshod over tea-break and test match. This is where you

Fig. 1.

have no wish to be but, ironically, where many a great stride in the furtherance of Anarcho-Dandyism can be made.

If you approach work in the right way, most of your day will be spent side-stepping the unreasonable demands of your 'superiors', stealthily spreading dissatisfaction amongst your fellow workers and subverting the office ethos of industrious toil. This will require the utmost finesse on your part and it is unlikely that you will receive much support from colleagues, who will be too fixed on short-term one-upmanship to have any clear understanding of concepts such as freedom, courtliness or aestheticism.

Subversion

Whilst earning 'a bob or two' at the company's expense, the endless days will seem pointless and unbearably oppressive unless you keep yourself amused by indulging in a few subversive japes. One popular method of doing this is 'keyboard sabotage'. Whilst your co-workers are out having lunch, grab yourself the nearest bottle of correction fluid and paint over the letters on typewriters and computer keyboards. It is then a relatively simple matter to superimpose your own cheery good luck message on the keys using a sheet of Letraset (Fig. 1). Although a skilled typist will not be slowed down by such a ploy, more senior members of staff less versed at the art of touch typing will be thrown into confusion, and the office will remain in a state of consternation for a satisfyingly lengthy period.

Instead of being combatative or surly with the management, be excessively (and suspiciously) bright and co-operative. Remember, the most subtle nuance of knitted brow or knowing smile can wreak havoc with a boss's self-confidence. You should never under-estimate the undermining effect that changing your stock response from servility to civility will have. It is highly recommended that at this point you make a careful study of the admirable evasive techniques adopted by Herman Melville's eponymous hero, Bartleby. Emulating this stoical character you should affect a single, impenetrable phrase that can be used in any situation. Bartleby's oft-repeated reply to any request was, "I would prefer not to," but this is probably a little too inscrutably negative for our purposes. How about an unnervingly effusive: "Sir, my enthusiasm knows no bounds." Here are a few examples of how the phrase could be incorporated into everyday office parlance.

Day 1: *Boss:* Smyth, you are hungover and dishevelled.

Employee: Naturally, sir. I am young. But my recuperative powers are legend and my enthusiasm knows no bounds.

Day 2: *Boss:* Smyth, you are late. See me in my office with your sales figures.

Employee: I would be delighted, sir. My enthusiasm for your warm solicitude knows no bounds.

Day 3: *Boss:* Smyth, you are fired.

Employee: Sir, my enthusiasm for your little witticisms knows no bounds.

Boss: No Smyth, I really mean it. You're fired.

Employee: A golden world of opportunity awaits. My enthusiasm knows no bounds.

Of course, as important as undermining the very foundation of corporate power structure is, it will mean next to nothing if you don't at the same time make a bid for the hearts and minds of your colleagues, or the *lumpen officetariat*. Don't, on any account, be discouraged by their despicable tendency to leave obscene anatomical Xeroxes in the copier or perky comic post-it notes on each other's computers. They know no better. Lead by example. Put long sultry afternoons to good use by photocopying reams of poetry by Baudelaire, Keats and Verlaine and distribute them surreptitiously throughout burgeoning in-trays, or scan them randomly into the hard drives of their computers.

Skiving

Fig. 2.

Remaining hunched over the copier is one way of frittering away many a happy hour in a manner that is not immediately apparent to 'team leaders'. Others will occur to you thick and fast as the days drag by. The most popular of these is excessive telephone usage. This can take the form of external calls to friends and relatives, which are relatively high risk, or internal calls to pretty young secretaries and receptionists, which are a lot lower risk and potentially far more rewarding (Fig. 2).

With the advent of computer technology, a whole new range of evasive techniques now lend themselves to those unsuited to 'knuckling down' and doing a fair day's work for a fair day's wage. The desperately vulgar medium known as the 'World Wide Web', is sometimes useful in this respect. As much as its chat rooms, virtual environments and 'sites' might repel you, visually they do have the distinct advantage of bearing an uncanny resemblance to the legitimate work that you were supposed to be getting on with in the first place. It is even rumoured that decadent poetry, biographical information on obscure aesthetes and cocktail recipes can be 'accessed' over the telephone in this manner, although this seems highly unlikely.

Fig. 3.

Another tried and tested ruse for avoiding productive labour is pretending to have a particularly virulent bowel complaint. This is usually guaranteed to elicit sympathy from management and co-workers alike and secures you uninterrupted 'quality time' in water closets about the building. Whilst there, indulge in a little pleasantist action, liberally sprinkling essences of bergamot and frangipani, which will give the subliminal message to all passing abluters that a time of change and hope is at hand. If you fancy a slightly more radical approach, you might even consider carrying with you a hairdryer. On particularly crisp, winter days, while the coast is clear, lavatory seats and other surfaces where denuded flesh is laid may be warmed to a temperature more suited to leisurely evacuation (Fig. 3). By this simple expedient, employees will be encouraged to spend more time in cubicular confinement where they may muse languidly over the detrimental effect on soul and psyche of vulgarity, competition and greed.

When all else fails, and a particularly important deadline looms (one that you find yourself

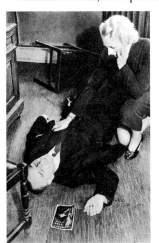

Fig 3. Feigning a fainting fit or serious illness remains one of the most reliable forms of work avoidance.

spectacularly unprepared for) there may be nothing else for it than to feign serious illness or a fainting fit. Tumbling off your chair and remaining motionless (Fig. 4) will in all likelihood gain you a reprieve until the following morning, by which time you may have been able to invent statistics or buy convincing documents from fellow workers.

It is a sad reality that even the stoutest of wills will gradually be broken by the system. As the weeks go by, deprivation of adequate lunch breaks, smoking areas and soft furnishings will start to undermine your revolutionary zeal. You may even find revolting terminology creeping into your office exchanges, such as 'ball-park figure', 'touch base' or 'do lunch'. This is nature's way of telling you that your tenure in the world of wage-slavery is at an end and it's time to get out. Any dilly-dallying at this point could prove terminal. Know your limits. Once you've earned an adequate amount to off-set your most pressing monetary needs hand in your notice, with victory in your eyes and air of louche superiority.

I WAS ON THE LOWEST RUNG of the criminal ladder – a common or garden 'tea leaf'. I did a bit of shoplifting, dealt in small amounts of Bob Hope, sold contraband salmon & trouts, half-inched mobile dog & bones, did the occasional mugging. Most of my takings went on cans of Forsythe Saga, doner kebabs, grub for the trouble & strife and the bin lids, bass bins for my Vauxhall Astra, and the odd line of Michael Caine down at Equinox, the local nightclub.

Then one day I tried to pickpocket one of your *agents raconteurs*. But he saw me coming, and the old Oliver Twist didn't work on him. When I got back to Beckham House, I went to pay my protection fee to the gang patrolling the estate, and found that *my* wallet had been half-inched!

I got a call later that evening from your agent. He invited me for a kitchen sink, saying he had a proposition to make me, and that he'd give me my wallet back. Well, the wallet had several rock 'n' roll cards under different names in it and I stood to lose out on £500 a week if I didn't get it back. When I met your agent in the local rub-a-dub, he offered to train me as a gentleman tea leaf, saying that the sums I could earn would make a monkey seem like peanuts. I agreed to his proposition and my training began immediately.

I was taught the codes of dress, carriage, manners and diction that would allow me to charm my way into high society. I was given instruction on how to locate the hostess' jewellery once I had been invited to dinner. I learnt to dance the quickstep, the foxtrot and the cha-cha-cha. This helped me gain access to the highest social circles in the country and soon I was invited on holidays to Monte Carlo, Nice and Monaco, where I applied the cheating techniques I had learned to games of blackjack and baccarat.

Now I am content to roam the world in the company of aristocrats and princes, none of whom suspect my origins. I am proud to say that my greatest acquisition has been a £10 note pilfered from Prince Charles' bedroom. This sort of amount would have been rich pickings back in my Beckham Estate days, and I keep it in the pocket of my Huntsman dinner jacket as a reminder of my humble beginnings.

About you

Surname (Hetherington-Farquhar

Other names Percy Cecil Harold Mary

Title Mr Mrs Miss Ms **Other title** Duke

1

2

3

Letters	Numbers				Letter

4 National Insurance (NI) number
Get this from payslips or papers from the Inland Revenue. Or get in touch with your social security office.

5 Are you able to work?
No ☐
Yes ☐

6 Are you willing to work?
No ☐
Yes ☐

7 Are you looking only for a temporary or casual job?
This might be because you
- are starting another job soon
- have been laid off
- have been placed on short-time.

No ☐
Yes ☑ Please tell us why. And tell us how long you want the temporary or casual job to last.

About work

I need plenty of free time to complete 'my life's work': "The Philosophy of Horse Racing: a Tragedy in 3 Acts"

8 What is your usual job?
If you do not have a usual job, write None.

Flâneur

9 What types of job are you looking for?
Please do not write Any. We need to know about...

Bon Vivant
Raconteur
Boulevardier
Man of Fashion
Wit
Man of Letters

Qualifications and work experience

13 Please tell us about any qualifications and work experience you have which will help you get a job.
We mean qualifications like
- degrees
- GCSEs
- O, A or AS levels
- City and Guilds
- NVQs, SVQs or GNVQs
- National Diplomas.

And work experience that may help you get the type of work you are looking for.
For example
- joinery
- building
- foreign languages
- computing
- typing.

While roaming around Turkey in my youth, I picked up a smattering of the local vernacular, as well as an understanding of the health risks involved in promiscuity — Alas, too late!

Having observed my little Egyptian factotum, Ahmed, at work around the home, I feel I have a rudimentary grasp of how to fill a cocktail glass and stoke a fire.

page 6

Abilities and interests

14 Please tell us about any abilities and interests which may help you get a job.
They could be things you do every day, outside interests or hobbies.

You may, for example, be good at
- making things
- organising
- selling things
- figures.

Or you may
- have a good eye for detail
- be very practical
- be understanding and patient
- be able to take care of people
- be able to work as part of a team.

I have a keen eye for spotting unsavoury types in a crowd. I feel that this skill, if developed with suitable training, may prove useful in a career as a spy.

I can also do a very clever trick with an olive, a cocktail stick and a maiden aunt's fox terrier.

15 Do you have a written summary of your skills, abilities and experience?
This is sometimes called a CV.

No ☑
Yes ☐ Please bring this to your interview.

page 7

More about work

Page 8 (top left form)

...an you start work as soon as you find a job?

You must be able to start work:
* immediately or
* at 24 hours notice if you do a service
* at 48 hours notice if you do voluntary work, or look after a child or adult.

Please tell us the reason. And tell us how soon after finding a job you could start work. ☑ No

It would take my tailor at least 10 weeks to make a suitable outfit.

17 What is the lowest wage you are willing to accept?

Tell us the amount before tax, National Insurance or anything else has been taken off. Do not include bonuses or overtime.

If the amount you put does not give you a good chance of finding work, your allowance may be affected. You can discuss this at your interview.

£12 guineas every ~~hour~~/day/ week / month / year

18 Are you doing any education or training?

No ☑   Yes ☐   Date ☐

For our use   18 ES 5675 completed   Initials

Where can you work? (page 10)

21 Which town or areas are you looking for work in?

Please be specific. Do not put *Anywhere* unless you are willing to work anywhere.

We need to know how far you are willing to travel to work.

Singapore
Cairo
Shangri-La
Xanadu
Arcadia
Polynesia
Nirvana

22 What vehicles are you licensed to drive?

None ☐   Car ☐   Motorbike ☐

Public service vehicle (PSV) or Passenger carrying vehicle (PCV) ☐
Heavy or large goods vehicle (HGV or LGV) ☐   Class ☐
Other *Horse* ☐

23 Do you have your own transport?

No ☐   Yes ☑ *– see above.*

camels
Elephant

Your efforts to find work (page 11)

24 Please tell us how you are going to look for work.

At your interview we will talk about your plans and what should be in your Jobseeker's Agreement.

If you are not sure how you are going to look for work, we can talk about it at your interview.

To find work I will

☐ Contact employers to see if they have any vacancies. *Hardly!*
☐ Visit or phone the Jobcentre to find and apply for jobs. *For God's sake!*
☐ Look in newspapers to find and apply for jobs. *There aren't any in the Racing Post.*
☐ Register with employment agencies – other than the Jobcentre. *Oh Please!*
☑ Ask family, friends and people I have worked with before about possible jobs.

Most of my family are either ~~raging~~ mad! or refusing to speak to me, but I believe there is one great uncle in Buckinghamshire whom they haven't locked up.

Improving your chances (page 12)

26 Please tell us if you need information about any of these things.

☐ Preparing a written summary of your skills, abilities and experience. This is sometimes called a CV. *I would call that a novel.*
☐ Writing letters to employers. *I'm one has worried me.*
☐ Filling in application forms.
☐ Doing well at interviews. *I do not have a telephone.*
☐ Talking to employers on the phone.
☐ Benefits for people in work, for example Working Families Tax Credit.
☐ Advice on starting a small business. *Why on earth would anyone start a small...*
☐ Advice on managing your job search if you have a ~~illness~~ *...business?* health problem or disability.

...anything ...d work and ...of finding

...of your ...rience ...jobs

Use the box below to tell us about any other help you need to find work or improve your chances of finding work.

If you could send someone down to the Coach & Horses at around 3 pm, I would be happy to accompany them to the French House. This, I feel, would considerably broaden my chances of finding work.

Your declaration (page 13)

I declare that to the best of my knowledge the information I have given on this form is true and complete.

I have read and understood the notes on this form.

Your signature _____   Date *MMI/V/XVI*

28 Please tick this box if someone filled in this form for you. ☑

Gordon's Gin

For our use

The adviser has read me the questions and answers on this form.

I agree they are true and complete.

Do not sign here unless we ask you to at your interview.

Jobseeker's signature _____

Date ___/___/___

A MEMO FROM SCOTLAND YARD
NETLEY LUCAS
CONFIDENCE TRICKSTER, FORGER, THIEF & GENTLEMAN
CASE STUDY NO. 3
SNUFF MOVIES

AN OFFICER AND A GENTLEMAN

NEW SCOTLAND YARD
FIGHTING NASTY CRIMINALS SINCE 1603

GENERAL ENQUIRIES **0234 456 789**
MISSING PERSONALITIES **123 345 6789**
LOST SOULS **124 567 876**
ALCOHOL PROBLEMS **999**

MEMORANDUM

To: All units in Great Britain
From: Sir Peter Condom, Super-duper chief top-boss inspector and long arm of the
Law in charge of everyone in the country who is a policeman

MEN, BEWARE

A new type of criminal is at work on our streets, wreaking havoc on society as we know it and leaving in its wake a spate of cheery *joie de vivre* and dry martini addicts. This criminal appears to be part of an as-yet undisclosed fringe political movement whose principal aims are to imbue society with high personal grooming standards, fine clothing and merry conviviality. As such they must be stopped immediately. Since the name of the political wing is not yet identified, we shall refer to this type of criminal as the Gentleman Criminal. He can be recognised by the following characteristics:

1. Immaculate dress sense: usually a Savile Row or similar suit; freshly-picked buttonhole; highly polished shoes. In short, a bit of a ponce.
2. Hair: cut short over ears and neck, plastered down with Brylcreem or pomade. Facial hair: occasionally pencil moustache or similar.
3. He usually works alone or in pairs.
4. Accoutrements include pipe, cigarette holder, hip flask, monocle.
5. Age: 21–55, could be younger or older, in fact could be any age.
6. Accent: clipped, brisk, pleasant, quaintly reminiscent of WWII fighter pilots.
7. Beware of concealed weapons, eg. cut-throat razor; hair dryer; sock suspender; sharpened brolly; small hammer; nail scissors; volume of Dada poetry.

There follows a brief outline of the crimes these revolutionary rogues have been perpetrating. Please note, none, repeat none have been arrested yet. I beg you all to try and arrest one of these buggers soon or we'll have a national scandal on our hands and plenty of egg on our faces.

GENTLEMANLY CRIMES

SHOP GIFTING

Time: day
Location: clothing stores
Victim: young, trendy consumers

This crime involves 'dropping' items in shops whose stock doesn't match the gentleman criminal's standards. The shop-gifter is usually active in high street chain stores such as Top Shop, Gap, etc. Targeting key display areas, he drops a choice item of clothing of his own on top of piles of store clothing, attaching an in-store price tag to it. The idea is that a customer will purchase said item in the belief that it really comes from the shop. Recent reports have indicated the dropping of pairs of sharply-creased grey flannels on to piles of combat trousers in Next.

CHARMED ROBBERY

Time: night
Location: traffic lights
Victim: married couple

The typical scenario is as follows. A man and his good lady wife are driving home after a pleasant evening at the theatre and they pull up at some traffic lights. Alongside their car a flashy convertible sports car pulls up, driven by a handsome rake in a houndstooth suit, matching driving cap and tan driving gloves. Within the few seconds before the lights change to green, the rake manages to persuade the lady to join him for a late supper at his bachelor flat in Pimlico, and the husband watches in horror as his wife steps out of his car and joins the rake in the sports car. Curiously, the victims of charmed robberies nearly always find that the stolen goods are returned the following day, more or less intact.

DRIVE-BY SUITINGS

Time: night
Location: city streets
Victim: youths in logo-heavy urban sportswear

It happens like this. A youth is on his way home after breakdancing at a nightclub. Suddenly an approaching car screeches to a halt. Two immaculately attired gentlemen leap out, they rugby tackle the youth to the ground and swiftly strip him of his Hillfiger and Nike. The tracksuit and trainers are then replaced with a Savile Row suit and a shirt, tie and shoes from Jermyn Street. The two gents bundle the youth's old clothes into the boot of their car and speed off, leaving him standing in the road, looking a sight better than he did before, despite being the victim of a heinous crime.

Other gentlemanly crimes being perpetrated are:
Assault & flattery and the illegal distribution of snuff movies.

NB: Any officers attempting to arrest one of these gentleman criminals please note: proceed with extreme courtesy. The gentleman criminal does not respond to violence. He will merely charm his way out of any such approach. Softly softly spoken, please – beat him at his own game. Adopt a Dixon of Dock Green stance: courteous, civil, respectful. This will confuse the gentleman criminal who, we understand, is trained to counteract aggression in all forms with resistant passivity.

Netley Lucas
Confidence Trickster, Forger, Thief & Gentleman

A LIFE OF CRIME *is always a viable option for anyone seriously interested in pursuing the cause of Chappism. Apart from the obvious benefits of not having to slave away in an office to earn a living, crime has the attendant cachet of glamour and sophistication to add to its appeal. One of the most exciting criminal career paths is that of the gentleman thief or confidence trickster. Here we recount the true story of Netley Lucas, whose dedication to these criminal pursuits is worthy of serious study.*

DETECTIVE INSPECTOR PERCY SMITH knocked on the door of a studio flat in the King's Road, London, at 10:15 am on 4th April, 1932. The door was answered by a charming young lady in a negligee. "Is Mr Lucas at home?" asked Smith. He was shown into the flat with his two officers and found a young man seated at the kitchen table, wearing a Japanese dressing gown and filling a meerschaum pipe. "Netley Lucas, I have a warrant for your arrest," said the Inspector.

"What are the charges?" asked the young man, lighting his pipe.

"You are charged with the falsification of Royal documents and earning monies through fraudulent business concerns under an assumed name."

"May I perform my toilet and have some breakfast before leaving?" enquired the surprisingly calm young man.

He was granted his request, and while he dressed and shaved, the young lady cooked him a light breakfast of eggs benedict and devilled kidneys. During this repast, the coalman arrived. When he'd deposited a hundredweight of coal into the coal-bin, he stood waiting next to the table.

"What do you want?" asked Netley.

"I want to be paid," he replied.

"Sorry, but I am in the process of being arrested, my good man," Netley continued eating his breakfast.

"You either pays me now, guv'nor, or I takes the coal back." Netley glanced at his scantily-clad lady friend, took out his chequebook and wrote the man a cheque, tipping him handsomely. When he'd finished his breakfast, he was led down the stairs to the street and put in the back of a police van with the two officers.

During the journey to Walham Green Police Station, Netley Lucas reflected on his career as a confidence trickster, thief and forger, and decided that he'd had a pretty good innings by anyone's standards.

EXPELLED FROM PUBLIC SCHOOL at 14 for forging the headmaster's signature, Netley Lucas drifted into a life of petty crime in the West End of London, soon making friends among the criminal fraternity. His youthful good looks, impeccable dress sense and familiarity with the upper classes made him a useful accomplice. The modus operandi was as follows. The crooks would enlighten themselves to the arrival in London of wealthy female visitors in possession of fine items of jewellery. Netley would then secure an introduction and charm the young lady over dinner with his dazzling looks and panache, ensuring an invitation to her rooms. While she was performing her toilet, Netley would lift the desired article from her jewellery case and later deliver it to his accomplices. To avoid arousing suspicion, he generally maintained contact with his victim afterwards, sometimes even assisting them in reporting the theft to the police.

Netley refined his art under the tutelage of 'Gipsy' Lee, a high-class crook with years of experience, who saw in the suave young Netley someone worthy of inheriting her mantle. She helped him gain membership to the most exclusive gentlemen's clubs in London, such as Oddemino's, the Piccadilly and the Berkeley, and taught him how to use his silver tongue to extract useful information from every casual conversation. By the time he was 18, Netley was maintaining the luxurious lifestyle of a society lothario through confidence tricks and theft, with only an occasional spell of 'durance vile' to interrupt it.

It was when his professionalism briefly deserted him that Netley nearly came a cropper. He had been assigned the task of stealing a pearl necklace from a celebrated French actress. He secured an introduction to her, and for weeks squired her around town after her theatrical appearances. When his accomplices began to show signs of impatience, Netley pleaded to be released from his assignment, for he had fallen in love with the actress. This was met with the grim-faced resentment typical of the criminal underclass, secretly envious of rare men such as Netley who are able to cross the Rubicon to the Bank of Dishonesty while maintaining a sophisticated lifestyle. They insisted that he procure the necklace forthwith, 'or else', which is quaint Cockney parlance for a dose of fisticuffs. Netley was assured that his most valuable asset, his visage, would be of no use to him after they'd finished with him.

Netley got the necklace and the actress returned to France, but the threat had unsettled him. During this time, he was masquerading under what were to be many aliases. The name of General Chilfont, a South African naval officer, enabled his entry into the most respectable ballrooms and drawing rooms. When Netley crossed paths with an acquaintance of the real General Chilfont, Scotland Yard were alerted to the impostor's activities. He was arrested while dining with a charming young lady called Phyllis. "I have nothing to say," he told the police officer. "Will you let me pay for my dinner and see that my guest has a taxi." Throughout his criminal career, Netley always held the officers of the constabulary in the highest regard. He believed they exemplified the British code of fair play and the majesty of British justice, and even though they often snatched him away from freedom, at least they behaved like sportsmen.

Netley emerged from his term in gaol with the firm resolve to go straight and used his charisma to establish contacts in Fleet Street. With his sharp mind and ready pen, he soon

made a name for himself on the dailies. The fledgling journalist was using his real name; it was precisely his exotic criminal past that his employers found attractive. One of the editors who gave him work took him under his wing and let him stay in his rooms during his frequent trips abroad. Netley allowed his past to catch up with him; he invited some former crooked friends around for a party and they promptly robbed the place. His benefactor returned, and Netley found himself on his uppers.

Netley's name became mud in Fleet Street, and he was reduced to seeking employment among the menial trades. This proved difficult, for the catering establishments he approached found it hard to believe that this exquisitely dressed young cove really needed a job as a washer-up. It was in the smoking room of the Cunarder Club that his fortunes changed. He overheard a conversation between two American publishers, one of whom was describing the difficulty he was having in gaining access to the King of Belgium's memoirs; he mentioned the kind of sum he would be prepared to pay to get hold of them. Netley decided there and then to act as King Albert's unofficial amanuensis. Within months he had secured a contract with a reputable publisher and, under the name of Evelyn Graham, earned himself a handsome advance fee.

From then on, Evelyn Graham's career as a biographer progressed apace. A plethora of biographies ensued, taking as their subjects such royal luminaries as Queen Mary, the Prince of Wales and King Alfonso XIII of Spain. He formed his own publishing company, Albert Marriott Ltd, employing writers to churn out the biographies, himself taking the role of editor and agent. His impeccable manners and well-cut clothes gave no-one reason to question his links with royalty and the aristocracy. If required to provide evidence of authorisation, he used his forging talents to create bogus letters, printed on Royal notepaper with an official seal. Netley had to be continually on his guard to avoid exposure. As an author and publisher, he was moving in similar circles to his career on Fleet Street, and the tiniest query or contractual hitch could have had disastrous results if it should lead to the revelation of his real identity as a former crook and gentleman con-man. There were two phones on Netley's desk, one to receive calls for Evelyn Graham, the other to answer as Albert Marriott.

Netley's amorous exploits were as steeped in duplicity as his publishing career. As is common with men of success, criminal or otherwise, he had a libido of unusual magnitude. A routine evening would run something like this. At 4 pm his chauffeur would collect him in a black Stutz Straight Eight from his offices in Egyptian House in London; he would take tea with one of his mistresses in Clarges Street; then he would be driven to Eastbourne to dine with his wife, whom he had installed in the Cavendish Hotel when their sexual relations had reached a plateau of indifference; thence to Rottingdean, for a late supper with his German mistress, Hanna, whom he kept in a bungalow there, and after that he would return to London, via a casino he liked in Brighton.

One day a journalist from the Daily Mail walked into the offices of Albert Marriott Ltd. Netley refused to see him, and instructed his private secretary, Dick Lampton, to keep him in the reception area, asking him to type his message on the sturdy Remington. The journalist did so, but immediately tore up the letter after typing it, and promptly left the building.

Fearing the worst, Netley had told Dick to insert a fresh piece of carbon into the typewriter. He was thus able to read the letter which the journalist had decided not to give him, imprinted on the carbon. It informed Albert Marriott that he was about to be exposed in the Daily Mail as Netley Lucas, the ex-convict behind the bogus Royal biographies written by Evelyn Graham. The net was about to close around Netley. He decided to flee the country before the Daily Mail put a match to the fuse.

Netley and Dick were aboard HMS Kilkenny bound for Durban, South Africa, when they spotted their visitor from the Daily Mail loitering around their cabin. When they reached port, Dick ostentatiously ordered two flights to Cologne, Germany, in the presence of the journalist. Daily updates were now appearing in the Mail on the whereabouts of Netley & Co, but with this ruse they managed to give the pursuing hack the slip, and they stayed on in Durban while he flew to Cologne. Netley and Dick spent their remaining funds on living the high life for a few weeks in Durban, knowing that when they returned to England it would all be over.

Netley returned to the UK, sold his possessions and went straight to the Official Receiver to declare himself bankrupt. In a calculated bid to bluff the Daily Mail, he marched into their offices and announced who he was. The editor told him that, while 'Netley on the Run' was a good story, 'Netley Returned' was not. Indeed, there is no record of Netley's activities for some time after that. He either kept his nose to the ground in a respectable job or restricted his criminal activities to something less worthy of media attention than bogus Royal biographies. Perhaps it was for the very reason that fame, glamour and notoriety were no longer his that he practically thrust himself into the hands of the Law, through an incident entirely unrelated to his former pursuits.

One night a man calling himself Leslie Graham called into Walham Green Police Station. He said he lived in a studio flat in the King's Road and sought police assistance on a sensitive matter. Apparently, he had been accused by a neighbour of running a brothel in his humble abode and he wanted to prosecute the neighbour for slander. The officer who spoke to Mr Graham thought his face was familiar, and as soon as he'd left, he consulted the Police Gazette, and satisfied himself that his visitor had been Netley Lucas, whose handsome visage was a regular on the Wanted list. The next morning, Detective Inspector Percy Smith paid a visit to the address in the King's Road given by Mr Graham.

 **WHEN THE POLICE** van arrived at Walham Green Police Station, Netley was put into a cell. He was allowed to make one telephone call, which he used to ring his turf accountant to place a bet on 'Gallant Folly' in the 2.45 at Epsom.

The trial of Netley Lucas lasted eight days, in a courtroom packed with society people and men of letters. In summing up, the judge, Sir Ernest Wild, said, "Never before have I met such an impudent scoundrel who has foisted on the public such trashy literature." Netley Lucas was sentenced to 18 months. While serving his sentence, he wrote his memoirs, which were published upon his release under the title of *My Selves*, by Netley Lucas and Evelyn Graham. The book was the only one of Netley's to become a bestseller, and he made a fortune from it.

Snuff Movies

EVER SINCE JEAN NICOT (the French ambassador to Lisbon and the fellow from whose name the ever delightful word 'nicotine' was derived) sent some tobacco leaves to the French queen, Catherine de Medici, in 1560 with instructions on how to use them as snuff to cure her migraine, the practice of tobacco inhalement has been planted firmly on the map of pastimes for those of a sophisticated or opulent turn of mind. The dandies and fops of the 18th and 19th centuries brought the practice to full fruition and developed complex rituals for the consumption of nasal confectionery (see Revolutionary Etiquette).

Tragically, the small-minded proclivities of public health advisers, coupled with an inexplicable lack of interest from the media, has led to a steady decline in its usage over the course of the 20th century. A middle-aged generation, dismissive of the ways of their forefathers, have cast snuff taking aside in favour of, at best, more conventional forms of narcotic such as cigarettes and alcohol or, at worst, the enforced vulgarity of gymasium and running-track. Thankfully, all is not lost. A thriving avant-garde of neo-foppists and languid aesthetes, heartily sickened by these conservative attitudes, and more than willing to try something new and exotic, are finally placing snuff-taking (or 'breathing the brown tiger' as the Chinese so picturesquely put it) back where it belongs, at the top of the list of stylish recreations for a young man. In gothic drawing rooms, perfumed boudoirs and clandestine snuff clubs across the land, sensitive souls gather to spend pleasant days greedily hoovering up impressive quantities of ground tobacco leaves.

A particularly exciting (and largely undocumented) aspect of this renaissance has been its impact on sections of the underground film-making fraternity. Made on extremely low budgets and never circulated outside a coterie of snuff aficionados, 'snuff movies' as they've come to be known chart the bizarre rituals, decadent decor and colourful characters that make up the intriguing world of snuffery. What opium was to Thomas de Quincy, alcohol to Charles Bukowski and mescalin to Aldous Huxley, so too is snuff to a growing band of cutting-edge auteurs.

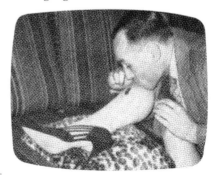

As far as we can ascertain, the first evidence of this new genre emerged in 1996 with the showing of *Mondo Nicotino* a film by American film-maker Willaby Fentash. A recent film graduate, Fentash was introduced to a snuff house in the borough of Hackney by one of his student chums and instantly fell under the spell of the exquisite wildlife and depraved brand of Englishman he found therein. Fentash uses a raw and powerful treatment of the subject, combining camp cabaret, well-built ladies of dubious moral rectitude and scenes of disturbing nasal abandonment. The film caused an uproar when it was first shown in a disused tobacconist down the Balls Pond Road and many critics still believe that the exaggerated picture it portrays has given a bad name to snuffdom, one that it is still trying to brush off.

The patchy reception afforded to *Mondo Nicotino* didn't deter two members of the audience that night, namely Auberon Tincture and Smedley Brace. Professional artists and inveterate partakers of snuff, they were enormously impressed by what they saw and decided that the time was ripe to make snuff the focal point of their next project. The result was *Nasal* (1997) a determinedly arthouse production, abandoning the hyperbole of the *Mondo* format in favour of an almost static plot line. "Snuff is the star. Snuff is the score. Snuff is the screenplay," Tincture has commented in one of his more forthcoming statements. It is not difficult to see what he means. The film lasts 185 minutes and for its entirety features a close-up of Smedley Brace's nose as he attempts to inhale two and half pounds of prime Café Royale. Their follow-up *Mucus Membrane* (1999), employs fibre optic lens technology to record to passage of snuff up the nostrils and into an eagerly receptive bloodstream. Both films have a mesmeric, if somewhat tedious, beauty.

Over the last few years, snuff movie production has exploded throughout Britain. Some of the more notable releases include, *Snorter House Five* (Hugo Flynt 2000) covering the olfactory adventures of five chums in Dresden during the Second World War, and *Hooter Scooter* (Willaby Fentash 2001), a seedy exposé of snuff dealing down the Charing Cross Road. Below we feature stills from *Pinch* a film by promising newcomer Roderick Makeshift. Makeshift's sparse and elegant treatment of a debauched weekend in a small farmhouse on the Pembrokeshire coast restores the dignity to snuff-taking that some of its more strident predecessors might have missed. With many a fledgling movie maker in the wings the future looks bright for independent cinema's most creative maverick sons.

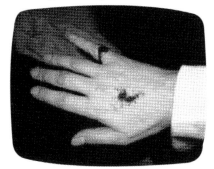

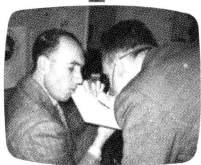

CASE STUDY:
The Story of 'Mark'

"I WAS WORKING as a software co-ordinator for a web-based global media network. It was mind-numbingly tedious work, but it was the kind of job that had cachet back then. It was all e-this and e-that. We were based in an e-loft in Shoreditch, everyone had their e-stations and had to fulfil certain e-initiatives on their e-portfolios. You would always be trying to outdo everyone else with how much jargon you could come out with. So you'd say things like, 'Guys, let's embrace frictionless infomediaries by meshing extensible systems and enabling cross-platform deliverables!' And the reply would be something like, 'Yeah, or how about incentivizing next-generation e-tailers by scaling collaborative niches?'"

Mark (not his real name) takes a long draught of his tall glass of absinthe, clearly shaken by the memory of his former life. He has agreed to meet us in this small tavern in Hellkinarny, Scotland, to share his story with us. "Then a chance meeting with one of your *agents raconteurs* as I was leaving the e-loft at 3 am one morning changed everything. Your agent happened to be on his way to a depraved gathering of louche individuals in a seamy bordello in that part of town, and he invited me to join him, I suppose sensing a soul in torment. It was incredible! In an oak-panelled private room in the bordello, we sat at a plain

table for some good home cooking – it was guinea fowl, I recall – washed down with a fine burgundy, before retiring to the library to smoke cigars and discuss poetry and philosophy. Not once did any mobile phones ring. In fact the entire evening was totally 'off-line', to coin one of my former e-commerce phrases. We were later joined by some very nice young Turkish boys, who engaged us in a species of parlour game. . . I seem to remember being offered a puff on hookah. . . Can't remember much after that, but it was a splendid evening, anyway. The next afternoon, I marched into the e-loft, and told them where to stick their frictionless infomediaries. I was about to leave a lethal virus on their network, but thought that'd be doing them a favour, so I just walked out."

Mark now runs a little inn on the outer Hebrides and he has been embraced by the local bohemian community. He is now president of the Philosophy Society and vice-president of the Early Music Club. He spends much of his time composing love poems that he hand-prints on hand-made paper in editions of three – one for himself, one for the British Library and one for the Police.

THE WELL-TEMPERED
PORTMANTEAU

ASPHALT REVERIES
THE DEPENDENT TRAVELLER
THE TRAVEL BUG

Asphalt Reveries:
The Discreet Art of Motoring

Fig. 1. Window boxes. A cheap and effective way to make your mark on the public highway.

IT MIGHT BE ASSUMED in these days of overcrowded roads and escalating fuel prices that the golden age of motoring is well behind us and, to a certain extent, that assumption would be true. Sadly a great deal of suspect mythology has grown up around the cult of the car, with boorish motor journalists obsessing about irrelevances such as fuel consumption, horsepower and the phallic symbolism of cars that seem to have all the design finesse of a plastic egg carton. But, with a little ingenuity and cogent planning, the motor car might still be freed from the grasp of vulgarians and fools, and reclaim its rightful place as a chariot to the sublime.

That ludicrously overpaid novelist, Mr Martin Amis, has defined a poet as "someone who doesn't drive". This might be pushing a point too far, especially when one considers the freedom from the horrors of public transport that motor travel engenders. However, it is true to say that ideally a Chap shouldn't have the foggiest idea what is going on under the bonnet of his car, and should be no more interested in the inner workings of the internal combustion engine than he is in the disturbing intricacies of the female reproductive system.

Automobile Aesthetics

As any Anarcho-Dandy knows, profundity can only be discovered in the surface of things, and when it comes to motoring it is the dash that you and your vehicle cut that is of prime importance.

When buying a car forget prosaic notions such as mileage, age, condition of the chassis, etc. and concentrate on the important things. That is, its colour, lustre, the presence of chrome and the aesthetic beauty of its bodywork. Automobile design has hit a bit of a nadir in recent years, and it seems likely that your basic requirements may only be fulfilled by a vehicle that pre-dates 1972, when the art of car design effectively died. An older car also has the advantage of travelling at sedate speeds more conducive to neo-foppist reverie.

Having made your purchase, you will gradually become aware that your cherished revolutionary beliefs are not common currency on the public highway. The prime motivation for a Chap to take to the road is, of course, to be seen and, in being seen, to act as a visual and highly mobile reminder that the forces of common courtesy still have a place on our city streets.

It is almost certain that you will find yourself at one time or other made an object of ridicule by local boy racers too dull-witted to understand the sanctity of your mission. This should only

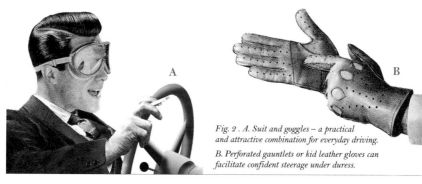

Fig. 2 . A. Suit and goggles – a practical and attractive combination for everyday driving.

B. Perforated gauntlets or kid leather gloves can facilitate confident steerage under duress.

have the effect of spurring you on to greater heights of aestheticism. During the warmer months cock a snook at bland convention by equipping your car with an attractive set of window boxes (Fig. 1). Hyacinths, aubrietia and tulips provide a colourful display from March to May and marigolds and lobelia create a charming effect during the summer season. It should be pointed out, however, that floral displays of this kind are only suited to short journeys about town. Hurtling along the fast lane of the M6 is not recommended for the propagation of exotic blooms and may prove ruinous to a lovingly nurtured herbaceous border.

Dress Code

So, you find yourself ensconced in the interior of a 1967 Triumph Vitesse convertible of an attractive off-white hue, a machine purring with aesthetic perfection. Surely the only question to ask is, "What on earth should I wear?"

The answer to this is clear and unequivocal. A sturdy three-piece suit tailored from a hardy fabric such as a 20 oz plain worsted. Such a cloth will protect you against the worst effects of inclement weather and rushing wind action. It is also common knowledge that the G-force of a speeding car can lead to sterility, but a pair of trousers of serious construction will act as an effective shield against such dangers.

To protect the face, even if your car happens to be equipped with the luxury of a windscreen, it is advisable to procure a large pair of motoring goggles (Fig. 2), which not only look dashing but also prevent the eyeballs from being dislodged when travelling on particularly uneven road surfaces. Leather headwear is an optional extra depending on one's personal preferences, but hair control may also be achieved by a copious use of brilliantine or by the wearing of a Solida 'Lord' gent's hair net (see Gentlemanly Requisites).

Correct purchase on the wheel is usually achieved by the use of perforated motoring gauntlets. These singular items strike the correct note between practicality and loucheness.

Taking to the Open Road

Slamming a car into first and taking her for her maiden voyage can be an exhilarating experience, but before you do so it is important to familiarise yourself with the essential controls and gadgets that are found in the interior of your vehicle. Study and memorise Fig. 3,

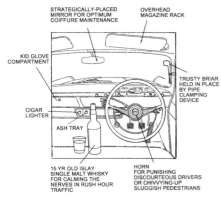

STRATEGICALLY-PLACED
MIRROR FOR OPTIMUM
COIFFURE MAINTENANCE

OVERHEAD
MAGAZINE RACK

KID GLOVE
COMPARTMENT

TRUSTY BRIAR
HELD IN PLACE
BY PIPE
CLAMPING
DEVICE

CIGAR
LIGHTER

ASH TRAY

15 YR OLD ISLAY
SINGLE MALT WHISKY
FOR CALMING THE
NERVES IN RUSH HOUR
TRAFFIC

HORN
FOR PUNISHING
DISCOURTEOUS DRIVERS
OR CHIVVYING-UP
SLUGGISH PEDESTRIANS

*Fig. 3. Familiarise yourself with the interior layout
of your vehicle prior to a maiden voyage.*

which illustrates the relative positions of the most important aspects of a car's interior design. There is nothing worse than finding yourself happily tootling along, only to discover that you have besmirched your legwear with cigarette ash, all because you haven't had the foresight to pre-locate the ashtray.

When embarking on a journey, concentrate on driving with consideration and courtesy for fellow drivers and pedestrians. The open highway has a fierce reputation as a breeding ground for naked hostility and mindless competition. It is all too simple to be drawn into this netherworld of squabbling and bickering. We advise you to avoid this at all costs. One course of evasive action is to equip your car with an ample supply of quality embrocation and heady narcotics. A moderate intoxication is usually guaranteed to mellow one's sensibilities to the foibles of other drivers. Although the consumption of alcoholic beverages is rumoured to be frowned upon by the authorities, in practice no officer of the law is going to prosecute a man who is found to be drinking a 15-year-old Islay single malt.

When it comes to dealing with pedestrians, a driver should be firm but fair. There is rarely anything more irksome than witnessing the feeble progress of a little old lady intent on crossing the road. This usually occurs at inappropriate points such as quiet back streets and zebra crossings that lull the elderly into a false sense of security regarding the dangers of peak-time traffic. With compassion aforethought, encourage old folk on their way by cheerily tooting your horn and revving your engine throughout the course of their passage. Having attained the safety of the opposite pavement, they will gratefully acknowledge your assistance with enthusiastic gesticulation.

Car Maintenance

And now to practical matters. As unbelievable as it may seem, due to ill-defined biological reasons, ladies are particularly susceptible to men who at least make a decent show of tinkering with a car engine. Science has no reasonable explanation for this phenomenon, but it's an effect that a Chap with amorous intent ignores at his peril.

This isn't to suggest that we all go out and attend evening classes in car maintenance. Perish the thought. But by the same token, being an Anarcho-Dandyist doesn't destine one to follow a path of Luddism or technophobia. The technology involved in the process of dry cleaning or the manufacture of the Corby trouser press, for example, can only be heartily endorsed, but the question is: should a fellow squander his intellect on notions of how these wonders of modern science might actually work? The answer, quite naturally, is 'No.'

The only route to follow is one of subtle intrigue. A man who knows on which side his

Right

UNCHARTED
TERRITORY

Wrong

ENGINE

*Fig. 4. The correct and
incorrect postures commonly adopted during car maintenance.*

concupiscent toast is buttered will adopt a selection of gambits designed to see him through even the most unexpected eventuality.

If you ever break down with a young lady on board, never panic. Admitting that you "simply haven't a clue" as to the cause of your trouble is not calculated to win respect. Instead, memorise a number of confidence building phrases, such as "By crikey, that carburettor will be the death of me" or, "Blimey, I told George that the fuel pump diaphragm needed seeing to." As you come grinding to a halt instruct your ladylove to remain within the car and disappear behind the open bonnet. From this point, hidden from observation, pretend that you are tinkering with the engine. Fig. 4 illustrates the correct and incorrect procedures for doing this. Note that the right-minded fellow on the left keeps his figure erect and firm, emulating the cut-and-thrust of motor mechanics by occasionally tapping his briar on the engine block and grumbling to himself as he does so. The foolish blackguard on the right actually endeavours to interfere with the inner workings of his automobile, forcing his spine into an awkward L-shape. Unnatural bending of this sort can lead to long-term injuries in the lower lumber region.

After a few moments of feigned enterprise, admit to your paramour that you, "think it's a little beyond my skills this time" and flag down a passing agricultural vehicle to take you to the nearest town or village, from where a brief call to the AA or RAC will turn a near disaster into a romantic adventure that will be cherished forever.

Having said this, there are some circumstances where displaying absolute ignorance of mechanical jiggery-pokery may be the only avenue open to you. There are certain men (and occasionally women) that pride themselves (by God knows what code of ethics) on an in-depth knowledge of engines. Feigning any level of expertise in such company only has the potential to cloak you with shame. Never be apologetic to such people. Clasp a slim volume of poetry to your chest, assume the loftiest of airs and reply to any questions in a manner you might reserve for responding to a query from a particularly impertinent cockroach.

"What do you reckon the trouble is?" sneers Hugo, knowing perfectly well that you've just run out of petrol.

"Haven't the faintest iota, dear boy," you reply haughtily. "I expect it's something to do with the engine." And then, extending a pale sensitive figure in the general direction of the closed bonnet, venture, "I believe it's in there somewhere."

The Dependent Traveller

ABROAD IS A STRANGE LAND where people do things very differently from us. While you may find it easy to procure such luxuries as opium, silk kimonos or a boy, you may find your attempts to locate a decent plug of mild shag absolutely impossible. Your holiday could be ruined beyond repair if, after the distressing upheaval of long-distance travel, you find you have forgotten to bring any moustache wax. To prevent such contingencies from arising, here are a few packing dos and don'ts, to ensure that you arrive Abroad with your portmanteau positively bulging with travel essentials.

Most young people in search of adventure will invariably pack several packets of **Rizla papers**, naively believing that spending their entire holiday in a marijuana-induced reverie gives them 'cool' or 'alternative' cachet. Nothing could be further from the truth. You'll look much more cool and alternative if you have a nice **briar pipe** with you at all times.

Guidebooks are seen as indispensable to the young traveller. Often referred to as their 'bible', these books are supposed to help them find the places where all the other young people are 'hanging out'. The reality is that they are excruciatingly dull to read and merely place you on an inescapable treadmill of annoying backpakers. Why not take **the Bible** itself with you? If at any time you feel threatened by the locals, you can read them passages from it. This will strike mortal fear into their hearts and they will probably believe you are some sort of deity. You will subsequently get the best table in every restaurant, and perhaps some nice presents left outside your hotel room.

Fleece jackets. The problem with this type of purpose-made utility wear is that it immediately singles you out as a wealthy member of the European elite, even if you are not, making you fair game for pickpockets. Fleece jackets also possess all the sartorial élan of a bowl of porridge. The **dinner jacket** is the universally acceptable dress of choice for men of all classes to spend the evening in. Thus attired, no one will make any assumptions about how much cash you are carrying, and you are far less likely to be targeted by thieving ruffians.

A Mosquito net is a rather cumbersome, ungainly and ultimately ludicrous travel accessory. Mosquitoes are known to actively avoid the skin of people who have consumed large quantities of quinine, which is one of the ingredients of tonic water. So all you have to do is keep yourself topped up with gin and tonic all day, and the hungry little bloodsuckers will leave you alone. The only type of net a Chap will need is a **snood**, a small net used to keep one's moustache tidy while asleep or drunk. The two straps slip behind the ears and keep every hair of the old fellow firmly in place, allowing for all sorts of indiscretions on behalf of its wearer.

Phrase books are seen as useful tools of communication with the locals when Abroad. Unfortunately, by the time you've fumbled your way through the pages to locate the appropriate phrase, the little street vendor you're trying to speak to has run off down an alley with all your money. It is far more practical, and enjoyable, to take a **riding crop**. Whatever language is spoken, you'll find that a few tactfully administered strokes soon get your message across.

Young travellers delight in exposing the virtues of their expensive **sandals**, whose manufacturer's spurious claims they have been fooled into believing. Most such claims focus on how well-protected, yet well-ventilated, the sandal-wearer's feet are, permitting him to wade through the most pestilent terrain while preventing athelete's foot. A **sedan chair** offers equal protection from the ravages of bacterial nastiness, and provides an excellent opportunity for refreshing the feet. While your footmen pant and heave at either end of the chair, you can put your bare feet up on the seat and lightly sprinkle them with talcum powder.

Credit cards. Young people these days like nothing better than to siphon off their student grants via cashpoint machines. These are unfortunately now available Abroad, which puts a huge strain on public resources, as students around the globe 'take a year out' and run up huge debts with credit card companies. A nicely printed set of **calling cards** is the only thing you will need to guarantee a safe passage through all foreign lands. These, coupled with a few notes slipped into the right hands and a letter of introduction, will instantly take you into the comfortable folds of diplomatic high society wherever you travel.

Torquil Arbuthnot
Explorer/philanthropist
Belgravia 361

The Travel Bug

JORIS KARL HUYSMANS informed us, in his novel *Against Nature*, that the only real way for a gentleman to travel is within the snug confines of his study, aided by nothing more than a bottle of absinthe and some travel-oriented literature. The Chap wholeheartedly concurs with such a view. However, if we are to implement the Charmed Uprising on a global scale, then as *agents raconteurs* we shall have to sally forth into that place known quaintly to the vulgaroisie as 'Abroad'. It is a sad truth that, since Huysmans' day, genuine foreign travel has lost much of its lustre. The blame can chiefly be laid at the sandal-clad feet of Youth, who have turned travel into a form of sport. The winner of the game of travel is the youth who returns from his globetrotting adventures with the largest amount of his parental allowance intact, and the most absurd collection of ludicrous jewellery, nonsensical hats and silly sarongs.

Many of today's youths invest six months or more of their precious time indulging their wanderlust. This period usually takes place between leaving university and entering the service of a large corporation. These callow youths often make a distinction between the 'tourist' (clean hotels, en-suite bathrooms, airport transfer, hot meals at regular intervals, guided tours of the essential cultural spots in a safe vehicle) and the 'traveller' (flea-ridden campsites, shared outdoor lavatories, meals shared on street corners with local peasants and their goats, exploring dangerous ghettoes on foot in search of undiscovered cultural 'gems'). It would seem infinitely preferable for a gentleman to be lumped in with the 'tourists' than to suffer the ignominies of the latter.

Many of our *agents raconteurs*, returning from reconnaissance missions to far-off lands, have brought back harrowing reports on the state of the non-indigenous Youth

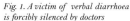

Fig. 1. A victim of verbal diarrhoea is forcibly silenced by doctors

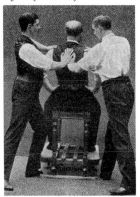

encountered there. These youths, it seems, have almost without exception been afflicted with one or more of the various perfidious travel bugs. They are in many cases so incapacitated by the symptoms that they are unable to fend for themselves, and their consul has to step in and make arrangements for their transport home. The bulk of these diseased youths tend to hail from three principal regions: Australasia, South Africa and Britain.

Fortunately, the CAD takes a great interest in afflictions of Youth, and at our headquarters in Pimlico we have devised various treatments for these travel bugs. Upon delivery of a sick youth to our centre by a roving agent, we can usually arrest the symptoms within a few weeks, and after a month or so we can either send the now healthy youth back into the world, or encourage him to join the Chappist cause and become an *agent raconteur* himself.

ONE OF THE MOST COMMON sicknesses affecting the long-term travellers is *verbal diarrhoea*. The symptoms are a complete inability to stop speaking about one's travels. Particular emphasis is placed by those afflicted on the incredible bargains they have found on their journeys. An unfortunate side effect is the adoption of an antipodean accent while recounting their tedious tales. A typical statement would sound like this, "Strewth mate, I was gitting a bid, brikfast, a tai chi lesson and an aromatherapy massage, all for one Australian dollar!" Once the sufferer has found a willing listener, they will literally not stop speaking of their travels until forcibly silenced (Fig. 1).

The cure is carried out within the gardens of our Pimlico headquarters. First we insist that the patient takes a vow of silence. After a few weeks of silent contemplation of the rich varieties of flora, and the sculptures of Apollo, Dionysus and Artemis in the gardens, the patient is permitted to say a few words, but only three at a time. We usually allow 'tea', 'pipe' and 'tobacco' to start with, to remind patients of their priorities in life. After several weeks of this, the patient begins to build up a normal vocabulary, and is able to master simple conversations on the day's selections in the Racing Post.

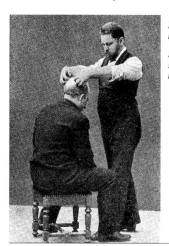

Fig. 2. (Left) Secondary treatment of cancer of the hair

Fig. 3. (Right) A particularly shocking example of the condition

A PARTICULARLY SHOCKING travel bug to behold is *cancer of the hair*. This rather nasty ailment affects both male and female travellers, and once it has taken root it can be very difficult to disguise, causing frequent alarm among the local indigenes. The symptoms of cancer of the hair are a series of stringy cankers that sprout from the scalp at random. They gradually thicken and become more bulbous until the entire head is covered in a thick, matted covering resembling a pile of rotting rope (Fig. 3). Fortunately the condition is not contagious, and treatment can be completed without isolating the patient.

The first stage of treatment is to entirely shave the head. The patient is then placed in a

small room every day, and music by Faure, Debussy and Noel Coward is played to his scalp while it is gently rubbed with brilliantine. The idea is to coax the hair back into a civilised shape. As it begins to grow, more brilliantine is added, a skilled barber is brought in to work on it, and slowly a proper short back and sides with a side parting is achieved (Fig. 2). Sometimes reading the poetry of Siegfried Sassoon can give the hair helpful hints on direction and style.

Fig. 4. This unfortunate case of sarong trousers was found in Bali.

ANOTHER HIGHLY DISFIGURING travel bug is *sarong trousers*. This is a nasty variant of the more common "wrong trousers", whereby unsuitable trousers, such as thornproof tweed, are worn in hot countries. Sarong trousers is much worse. The trouser legs fuse together into a single tube of flimsy cloth, usually printed with a vulgar batik design (Fig. 4), and the sufferer finds it increasingly difficult to walk properly, hobbling along like a geisha girl until they tumble to the ground to the amused delight of the locals.

The cure is mainly psychological. The patient must be re-taught the duality of his trousers, having become accustomed to encasing them in a single sheath of cloth (Fig. 5). Polo lessons are given, during which the patient can clearly observe his jodhpur-clad legs dangling on either side of the saddle. A visiting tailor is also used in the treatment. He takes the patient's inside leg measurement every day, and gradually the patient learns that his trousers consist of two legs of durable moleskin, and not one square of tie-dyed cotton.

Fig. 5. A victim of sarong trousers is reminded of the duality of his trousers.

Office Gambling · Dressing for Wrestling
Dressing for Tennis · Semiotics of Smoking

THE DIGNITY OF LEISURE

Office Gambling

THERE IS NO QUESTION that one of the most pleasant, diverting and downright sophisticated leisure activities that a Chap can participate in is gambling. What could be more thrilling than a day at the races, for example? Your finest country tweeds will get an airing, green trilbies are practically *de rigueur*, and there is really nothing quite so sensuous as the sound of hooves pounding on damp turf and the sight of a steaming nag, positively glowing with victory as it is led into the winner's enclosure.

It is well-documented that the ladies are inexorably attracted towards those men who dare to stake all on the throw of a dice, a fact perhaps connected to primitive nurturing instincts. Look at Neolithic man's heroic attempts to feed his family by hurling himself into the path of a mammoth armed only with a tiny club. Now observe the heroic gambler, who takes on the mighty odds stacked against him by trying to turn the housekeeping money into a fortune at the roulette table. What sight could arouse more pride in a lady than her husband, immaculately attired in white dinner jacket, bow tie and red buttonhole, a devil-may-care grin crossing his otherwise imperturbable face, as he hurls his month's wages on to the number nine?

But before you hot foot it down to the nearest casino, a word of warning. While the casinos of Monaco, Nice and Monte Carlo are still places of inherent charm and sophistication, the casinos of poor old Blighty have suffered something of a downturn in recent years. This can be attributed to the rather draconian gaming laws (the recent adoption of the euphemism 'gaming', as opposed to the more robust 'gambling', with its connotations of vice, corruption and scandal, speaks volumes). The result is a rather tacky atmosphere in today's English casinos, whose clients tend to be either middle-aged Arab

millionaires, or lottery-winners from the home counties on 'Spend, Spend, Spend' weekends in the capital.

So, apart from the as-yet-unspoilt pleasures of the race track, where is a gent to go when he fancies a flutter? The answer is simple: nowhere. Gambling is an activity that, with a little imagination, can be done anywhere at all. And what better place to start than that bastion of boredom, inertia and restlessness, the workplace?

The modern office, with its complex hierarchies, its numerous gadgets and gizmos and its large numbers of staff, is the ideal place for an infinite variety of gambling pastimes. Most office workers, far from cherishing any real interest in the products or services peddled by their employers, would like nothing more than to burn the place to the ground and dance naked around the flames in a drug-induced state of nirvana. While Chappism fully endorses this somewhat Latin American approach to subversion, we can suggest several more subtle ways to aggravate the corporate structure, while frittering away a pleasant afternoon of gambling at the same time.

Courier Racing

Select a simple journey visible from the office windows, say, once around the block and into the newsagents, then order several couriers from different companies to deliver parcels to fictitious places on this route. Set up race meetings between rival courier companies. Invite your colleagues to bet on which courier will complete the journey first. Let them 'study the form', if they wish, by checking previous records of deliveries by the various couriers. Motorcycle couriers are the most entertaining to watch, and the thrill of observing them speeding along the streets around the office is unparalleled. You can even visit the 'stables' of the courier company to have a look at their thoroughbreds and examine the sort of bikes they use. Note that it is unwise to let the couriers know they are racing each other. Like greyhounds chasing a mechanical hare, they perform better under the belief that they really are delivering urgent parcels.

Meetings Roulette

Meetings are always dull, tedious affairs, whose only redeeming quality is the temporary removal from your workstation. Liven them up by playing this variation on roulette. Instead of betting on which number will come up when the wheel is spun, get your colleagues to lay wagers on which words or expressions will come up in meetings. Choose the most inane, meaningless bits of corporate jargon currently tripping off the tongues of the most idiotic middle managers. Acting as croupier, take into the meeting a similar chart to the one printed below (the non-betting people at the meeting will assume it is some sort of sales figures chart). Before each item on the meeting's agenda is discussed, invite your colleagues to place their bets. You can avoid detection by using, instead of piles of banknotes, a hand-written number showing the amount to be wagered next to the selected word. The resulting chart when play begins will look something like this.

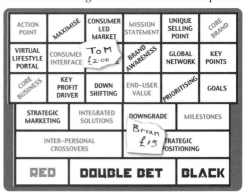

ACTION POINT	MAXIMISE	CONSUMER LED MARKET	MISSION STATEMENT	UNIQUE SELLING POINT	CORE BRAND
VIRTUAL LIFESTYLE PORTAL	CONSUMER INTERFACE	ToM £2·00	BRAND AWARENESS	GLOBAL NETWORK	KEY POINTS
CORE BUSINESS	KEY PROFIT DRIVER	DOWN SHIFTING	END-USER VALUE	PRIORITISING	GOALS
STRATEGIC MARKETING	INTEGRATED SOLUTIONS	DOWNGRADE Brian £15	MILESTONES		
INTER-PERSONAL CROSSOVERS			STRATEGIC POSITIONING		
RED	DOUBLE BET			BLACK	

Fax Racing

Best accomplished in very large companies with multiple departments and several floors, this involves two similar faxes being sent from opposite ends of the building to the reception desk, or 'winning post'. The fax must pass through all departments, or 'hurdles'. Before the race, canvas the entire building for bets on which fax will get there first and write up the odds on a notice board. The winner will have to show confirmation slips from all the designated fax machines and any discrepancy could result in a 'photo finish'. For example, a photograph of Simon in accounts, holding the fax aloft, will have to be seen to prove that the fax really did pass through his office. The same game can be played by e-mail, though this leaves more room for cheating, and there is a risk of accidentally forwarding the message to the MD's inbox.

Bartlebying

Based on the fictional character Bartleby (see *The Shirk Ethic*), this is a game played between two temps, which the full-time members of staff can bet on. The objective is for both temps to remain entirely inactive for the duration of their assignment. They achieve this by maintaining an inscrutable 'poker face' whenever asked to do anything. Any actual work done loses points and the stakes can be raised by taking extremely long lunch breaks. These can be matched by their opponent taking monumental tea or cigarette breaks. The winner is the temp who has not done a stroke of work and yet possesses a time sheet that will generate a full day's pay.

Dressing for Wrestling

WHILE BOXING HAS SADLY strayed irretrievably far from the civilised pugilism of the Queensberry Rules, the art of wrestling still possesses a classical nobility, evocative of the scantily clad warriors of ancient civilisations. Think of Oliver Reed and Alan Bates wrestling by a roaring fire in the film *Women in Love*, naked as Cro-Magnon men, and almost as hirsute. As gentlemen of action poised to overthrow the status quo, wrestling can be a good way to practice techniques that will help us outwit the truncheon-wielding constabulary, and make us a match for the most highly trained of the government's militia. It can also be a diverting way to while away a cool spring afternoon.

But before stepping into the wrestling arena, it would be wise to give due consideration to what we shall wear. There is nothing quite so vulgar as a grown man dressed in a purple Lycra leotard, and thus attired we can hardly expect to be taken seriously by our foes.

When dressing for wrestling, there is no reason to suspend the style judgements of civilian life. The suit has always been the most comfortable, universally acceptable form of male attire, so why leave it in the changing room? However, a word about contours. You would be unwise to step into the ring in a pair of Oxford Bags, however formidable they may look at the local tea dance. A double-breasted suit would also be a mistake – let us investigate why.

The sport of wrestling involves many grabbings, tossings and huggings (in this, and only this, it is not dissimilar to the sport of love-making). Hence the inappropriacy of anything

too loose, baggy or with tassels. You don't want your opponent grabbing you by the scruff of anything, so your most powerful sartorial weapon is simplicity. Choose the sleek lines of a suit from a decent tailor such as Henry Poole or Doug Hayward. Do not consider anything other than a single-breasted three-piece. The waistcoat is a vital place for you to store the end of your tie, an easily grabbed though essential accoutrement to any gentleman's attire. Not even in your most savage moments should you consider removing your tie. The same goes for cufflinks – just make sure they are not of a vulgar size, as you may find they are a convenient place for your opponent to get a purchase on your sleeve.

In some primitive cultures, such as the USA, a mask is worn in the wrestling arena. This is a highly advisable accessory. The mask has two main functions. Firstly, it keeps the hair out of trouble. A follicular tug can be rather painful, and may displace the sleek harmony of your brilliantined barnet. Secondly, a mask can intimidate your opponent into mistaking you for an evil pinhead sort who favours painful sexual practices and is not, therefore, to be trifled with in the ring.

Finally, a word on footwear. High boots with many lace-holes can be fun and will help consolidate your above-mentioned fetishist image. Shiny ones in black or red leather can, combined with your mask, strike such terror into your opponent that he is psychologically beaten before you lay a hand on him. However, a nice brown brogue will go much better with the suit if it is of a light colour; a black Oxford for the darker suit. If you prefer to continue with the S&M theme, try a brogue in a racy colour such as tan or burgundy, or show your opponent you really mean business by wearing a suede brogue.

Dressing for Tennis

REGARDED BY MANY as the most fashionable sport of all, tennis should be played in crisp whites, with a sharp crease on both trouser leg and shirt-sleeve. During inclement weather, long trousers may be worn, though extra care must then be taken to maintain the crease. This is best achieved by spending as little time as possible on the court; games can be limited to three sets instead of five, upon completion of which the players should repair to the bar. A visit to the bar prior to the game will put the players in excellent spirits, and will relieve the competitive tension, thus making the game more leisurely and devil-may-care.

Left: Tabs, snout, Harry Rag – call them what you will, cigarettes are a welcome complement to any young fellow's tennis clobber. A half-smoked fag dangling insouciantly from your serving hand throughout the game will give your opponent the right signal, "I couldn't give a damn whether I win or lose, old chum."

Left:
Collar position – CORRECT

The collar of one's white tennis shirt should never come higher than the bottom of the Adam's apple. This fellow manages to get away with unkempt hair, thanks to the wisdom of his collar position.

Right:
Collar position – WRONG

A raised shirt collar, especially during tennis, has hoi polloi written all over it. Leave this sartorial obscenity to those who take sport seriously, such as rugby players and rowers.

The Semiotics of Smoking

WHILING AWAY THE VAST tracts of time that lie between dawn and dusk should never present itself as a problem to a Chap of imagination. Lengthy bouts on the chaise longue coupled with elaborate grooming rituals should be adequate to fill most of one's waking hours, but sometimes a fellow may be inspired to experiment with leisure pursuits of a slightly more demanding nature. One such pastime is the semiotics of smoking.

A Chap with a cigarette, cigar or pipe in hand, when keenly observed, will within a matter of minutes unwittingly divulge not only his social status and current state of mind, but also vital information about temperament, reliability, employability, marital status, sexual proclivities and prowess, family background and literary tastes. Much pleasure may be gained by sashaying through the throng or dallying in public houses, notebook in hand, attempting to build up detailed psychological profiles of one's fellow man. Non-smokers who hold no truck with the tobaccotine arts have already revealed themselves to be beyond contempt and are therefore worthy of no serious consideration.

With this brief guide, the layman will merely be able to scratch the surface of a science that is as frighteningly deep as it is majestically long, but with a little application and additional research he will find the semiotics of smoking an invaluable insight.

The Impotent or Cuckold

An ostentatious panache can sometimes mask the grief caused by a wife's philanderings but this fellow's multiple cigarette usage coupled with an awkwardly affected smoking technique speak volumes about his inadequacies in the trouser department.

The Pub Politician

From time to time a fellow can be gripped by an urge to put a point forcefully. Although usually of vulgar usage the 'two-finger prod' can be highly effective in driving an argument home especially when debating with members of the lower orders.

The Nouveau Riche

Trying too hard is a social faux pas virtually impossible to excuse. The unattractive affectations of lottery winners and self-made persons of trade are the tell-tale signs of social inferiority and as such can have no place in polite society.

The Senior Man

The man who is happily assured of his own worth can decently allow himself the luxury of a less than overtly masculine smoking technique. Generations of seniority have left him oblivious to the taunts of the hoi poloi.

The Empire

Contemptuous of modern concepts of democracy and self-determination, 'The Empire', whilst rendering a man seductive and charismatic, should best be avoided as it has been known to lead to acute muscle fatigue and fisticuffs.

The Decadent Schoolboy

From its modest beginnings behind school bike sheds this grip has steadily become a national institution in areas where mis-guided authority has contemptuously disregarded a man's fundamental right to smoke. ☞

The Exquisite

Now almost exclusively the preserve of young women in the lower echelons of advertising and homosexuals, this classic stance deserves wider currency as a signifier of a singularity of mind and a certain opulence of the soul.

The Closet Lothario

This ineffectual-looking cove may look like the boy next door, but a closer inspection of his expertly cupped hand reveals a cunningly concealed prophylactic. The man is obviously an animal.

The Rum Cove

There is a certain brand of wilful contrariness that is often the result of inbreeding or an art college education. The aspiring host should think very carefully before inviting 'creative' persons to dinner parties.

The Extrovert

This fellow has clearly taken leave of his senses. In a miscalculated bid to court the attention of his chums, he has taken the noble pursuit of smoking and thrown it in the mire. He should never be trusted with any position of authority.

The Overly Considerate

Efforts to pander to the prejudices of the non-smoker will only earn you the opprobrium of all right-thinking people. A man who smokes with confidence and pride will find himself both respected by his colleages and admired by the ladies.

The Pervert

This blighter seems to be wearing women's clothing. If it weren't for the fact that he smokes Dunhill Internationals and that his father owns half of Carmarthenshire he would find himself excluded from all but the most 'theatrical' of cocktail parties.

The Sobranie

These young blades express a natural and healthy friendship through a shared enjoyment of Sobranie Cocktail cigarettes. A public school education has trained them to be at ease with male camaradarie and make the most of their bachelor days.

The Nonchalant, or Sloven

The subtle art of 'long ashing' should be attempted by none but the most experienced of smokers. A crucial combination of poise, steely nerves and split second ashtray technique make all the difference between universal admiration and ignominy.

COMTE DE MONTESQUIOU ■ ENEMAS FOR PLEASURE

COOKING WITH YOUR CORBY TROUSER PRESS

EXQUISITRY OF THE
CHAISE LONGUE

Cooking With Your Corby Trouser Press

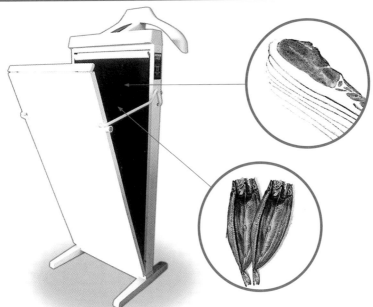

LYING ABED TILL NOON is surely the fundamental right of any man with a modicum of poetry in his soul, but late nights at the gaming table or bordello are liable to leave a fellow feeling as ravenous as a prime stallion just on the wrong side of his lunchtime appointment with the nosebag. Even those of limited logical faculties will see that these facts leave us struggling in the jaws of a pressing dilemma. In the absence of mewling staff to cater to one's every unnatural need (no doubt due to one being cut off without a penny by one's unimaginative parents) we find ourselves in the uncomfortable position of either having to rise and shine or, alternatively, go hungry. But wait a minute. Don't despair. One glance into the corner of your perfumed bed-chamber may provide an answer.

The Corby Trouser Press is without a doubt the most useful electric appliance known to mankind and it therefore seems criminal that this technological marvel is only put into action for the mere two hours a day that are required to keep one's trouser creases crisp and cheeky. With a small amount of resourcefulness, preparation and planning, this paragon of the modern age may be converted in a trice into a handy cooking implement for impromptu snacks, informal business luncheons or breakfasts with friends. 👉

Technical Preparation

Although your trouser press gives off a steady and practical heat for the maintenance of legwear, it does not necessarily make the wattage ideal for the preparation of foodstuffs. It is highly recommended that you first consult a professionally qualified electrician to peruse your appliance and, if necessary, tinker with its resistor in order to produce a heat compatible with culinary as well as sartorial needs. Also, the timer should be adjusted so that your press can remain switched on for several hours on end, to enable a thorough cooking of your comestibles. It should be borne in mind that a badly cooked kipper fillet is as offensive to the taste buds as an inelegantly turned out lady is to the eye.

Planning and Accoutrements

As familiar as you may or may not be with the usage of saucepans, frying pans and other cooking paraphernalia, you will find that trouser press cuisine involves the acquisition and utilisation of a new and exotic range of culinary hardware. It may be stating the obvious, but a trouser press does not allow much by way of a third dimension, i.e. it doesn't matter whether your chosen comestible is expansive in height or width, but depth is crucially of the essence. It is therefore necessary to gather together the following items.

1. **One hot-water bottle.**
2. **A foil bag retrieved from the interior of a used wine box.**
3. **A roll of kitchen foil.**
4. **A slim hip flask or cigarette case.**
5. **One roll of sturdy twine.**
6. **A pair of gardening or oven gloves.**

We should take one moment at this point to consider that trouser press cuisine is more than just cooking, it is a philosophy, an art, a spiritual quest. It not only represents a desire to combine eating well with a man's fundamental right to snooze, but also embraces issues relating to personal freedom, the blighting effects of paid labour and the never-ending search for inner truth. Some say, "We are what we eat," but the Chap says, "How we cook is how we think."

Resourcefulness and Technique

Now let's get down to basic cooking techniques. In the absence of copper-bottomed saucepans and other extravagant kitchen jiggery-pokery, a fellow has to fall back on boy-scout resourcefulness to broil, poach and simmer his prey into submission. Without too much effort, it is possible to graze the shelves of one's local grocers or supermarket in search of items flat enough for our purposes. Boil-in-the-bag items such as kipper fillets, gammon steaks, microwave rice and frankfurters are particularly useful in this context. They can be placed directly into the gentle jaws of your press with no further preparation necessary. However, other items such as rashers of bacon, asparagus, baked beans, fresh vegetables, tapioca pudding, creamed rice and coffee and tea require a little more thought. This is

precisely where your hot-water bottle and other requisites come into play. Through trial and error you will come to find the particular practices that suit your personal tastes, but a brief outline of cooking techniques follow:

1. For beverages such as **tea** and **coffee**, use a hot-water bottle (tied to the top of your trouser press with the aforementioned sturdy twine) half-filled with boiling water, two teaspoonsful of tea or coffee and leave to simmer for roughly eight hours. Exotic sauces may also be prepared in this way.

2. For **diced vegetables** a similar technique to the one above is used, but the disused interior of an old wine box (carefully modified with a pair of scissors to increase access) creates a suitable environment for lengthy simmering. Due to the fiddly nature of peas these may be cooked within the confines of a slim hip flask, the contents being shaken out moments before consumption.

3. **Asparagus** and **bacon** are best wrapped in foil to contain their juice flow. It is imperative that a firm seal is achieved, as accidental seepage is quite likely to prove ruinous, not only to one's trousers but also, consequently, at some later date, to one's self-esteem and one's chances of passing on one's genetic make-up to an enthusiastic recipient.

Let's Cook

The nature of your gathering – a light repast on one's own, a romantic breakfast *à deux* or a high-powered meeting with your turf accountant – will determine the extent of the cooking times and trouble you go to. For efficient timing it is suggested that an electrical timer switch is used to start off the cooking process, particularly if you happen to be miles away losing your shirt on the roulette tables at the time.

For a solo breakfast after a heavy night on the town, we heartily recommend a simple boil-in-the-bag kipper or a lightly poached egg *à la boule d'eau chaude*. Either of these, combined with a strongly stewed cup of coffee and a previously prepared Bloody Mary (kept chilled in a thermos flask) will make rising at around 2 pm a pleasure rather than a chore.

If you plan to breakfast in the company of a beautiful lady it might be a good idea to include asparagus, smoked salmon and scrambled egg on the menu, the latter being prepared by a vigorous shaking of the hot-water bottle prior to insertion in the trouser press. Accompanied by chill box items, such as a bottle of Bollinger and an oyster or two, this may just preclude the necessity for you to rise until early evening just in time to catch a fashionable cocktail party or two.

Meals for business associates or formal gatherings require a little more planning. For example, if you intend to receive foreign delegates or potential parents-in-law, presentation becomes more of an issue. Perhaps you should consider remaining fully clothed from the night before, so that your formal attire counterbalances the insouciant implications of your recumbent posture. Complex and sophisticated trouser press recipes such as *saucisson au pantalon* and *bacon gusset provençal* will require the dexterous use of several hot water bottles at once, but will immediately reassure all and sundry that, despite your poetic soul, you are a man worth doing business with.

Comte Robert de Montesquiou-Fezensac

THE COMTE DE MONTESQUIOU was the undisputed high priest of decadent European society and his reputation still shines like a beacon of exquisitry from *fin de siècle* Paris. If we are to learn anything about interior decoration, we must begin our journey with a visit to the Count's mansion on the Bois de Bologne, whose contents, as well as its singular occupant, were the inspiration for JK Huysmans' novel *Against Nature*.

At the front door of the Pavillon, we are greeted by Montesquiou's faithful companion and personal secretary, Gabriel d'Yturri, a short, handsome Argentine with bright brown eyes in a smooth, olive-skinned face. Somewhat mystified at the curious odour of rotten apples and chloroform that this young factotum gives off, we follow his flapping coat-tails into the darkened corridor, decorated with numerous paintings by celebrated artists of the day, such

as Gustave Moreau, James McNeill Whistler and Odilon Redon.

D'Yturri invites us first to contemplate the bathroom, of whose decoration the Count is said to have a particular fondness, and he leads the way up the stairs.

A glass cabinet flanks one of the bathroom's turquoise walls, in which reside 100 pastel-hued cravats. Though "mossou le comte" as d'Yturri fondly refers to his employer and mentor, is never seen without a crisp cravat decorating his throat these, we are assured, are but a fragment of Montesquiou's collection and purely exist for his personal perusal whilst engaged in performing his toilet. The 18th century pink marble bath was found by our charming guide himself, in the garden of a Versailles convent. "I paid for it with my own cast-off slipper," d'Yturri confides, "allowing the nuns to believe it had once belonged to the Pope." The young fellow will clearly go to any lengths to win the Count's favour. Water is issued into the bath via the lapis lazuli trunk of a porcelain elephant. A string of bronze monkeys linked by their outstretched arms serves as a bell to communicate with the servants.

D'Yturri informs us that the coolness of the bathroom's blues and pinks have prepared us sufficiently for what is known as the 'Snow Chamber'. Before entering, he takes from his pocket a charming fur hat and clasps it over his ears. He ushers us into the room and we are greeted by dazzling white decoration. A polar bear rug covers the floor, stalactites carved from glass and mica hang from the ceiling and a full-sized sleigh, draped with blue fox furs, sits in the centre. "I always feel f-f-f-frozen when I come in here!" d'Yturri announces in his almost perfect French.

We have been provided with felt slippers to view the upper floors. We are further requested to maintain absolute silence as we pass the Count's bedchamber, where Montesquiou is taking his afternoon nap, aided by his favourite post-prandial tincture of laudanum. The corridor is festooned with curios from around the globe: a stuffed marmoset; a Persian hookah; Japanese kakemonos; a marble Venus pulled by dolphins; Byzantine monstrances; ornate vases bursting with peacock feathers. As we descend the elegant staircase, d'Yturri points out the empty space on the wall where, until last week, there hung a painting by the impressionist Jaques Emile Blanche, a former friend of the Count's. The naive young artist made the cardinal mistake of inviting Montesquiou to dine with himself and the composer Fauré, omitting to mention that also present would be the Prince de Sagan, a deadly enemy of the Count's. It was tacitly understood that this marked the cessation of Montesquiou's friendship with Blanche, and he endured a final meeting with him to return his letters, handing them to him in a scented coffer of sandalwood. D'Yturri adds with relish that, having been the subject of malicious rumours about his relations with the Count, he had himself challenged Blanche to a duel. "It was for the master's honour that I was prepared to take up the sword," he asserts, clasping his hand to his heart and striking a pose in front of a splendid Chinese tapestry on the vestibule wall.

Next we enter the Empire salon, where the Count's favourite artworks are housed. The walls are filled with such a collection of aesthetic styles that we are thankful for the amenable presence of d'Yturri, who points out some of the more significant acquisitions. There are several very agreeable portraits of respected figures from the world of belles lettres, including the Goncourt brothers, Mallarmé, Verlaine and Huysmans, all of whom, we are reminded, are acquaintances of the Count. D'Yturri glows with a palpable sense of pride when showing us a portrait of himself by Boldini, resplendent in cycling cap and breeches. While he recounts the tale of Montesquiou organising the execution of the portrait by a leading impressionist of the day, one gets a glimpse of the devotion which seems to exist in equal measure between the Count and his secretary. It does not seem to be a purely employer–employee relationship; nor does it have the air of crude physical abuse of the servant by the master. It is certainly not common to see portraits of manservants, however exotically attractive they may be, within the houses of aristocrats. Neither is it common practice for employers to suggest alterations to their servants' surnames (in this case the Count suggested adding d' to the boy's original Basque surname of Yturri).

Several generations of Montesquious surround d'Yturri's portrait, recalling Edmund de Goncourt's observation that the Count possesses "that supreme distinction which characterises aristocracies when they are on the verge of disappearing." On a Doric plinth is a plaster cast of the Comtesse de Castiglione's feet, whose perfection had also been noted by the Emperor Napoleon III. While contemplating a drawing on the next wall by La Gandara of the Comtesse Greffulhe's chin, we silently note that, while the Count is believed to have vomited for an entire week after spending the night with Sarah Bernhardt, he is certainly no stranger to the charms of the female form.

Our eager guide has one more treat for us before tea is served. We are honoured by a rare audience with the Count's valet, a rather foppish young Arab fellow by the name of Mahomet. He takes us on a brief tour of Montesquiou's wardrobe, regaling us with various anecdotes connected to the astonishing array of costumes. We are shown the white velvet suit which the Count wore to one of his salons, outdoing the spectacularly attired ladies by sporting, instead of a cravat, a posy of parma violets at his throat. At one of the Count's many lectures, the audience eagerly anticipated an eccentric costume of some sort. But to everyone's astonishment, he appeared in a sombre black suit, looking like a solicitor's clerk. "The feeling I decided to arouse," the Count had explained to Mahomet, "was a disappointed expectation of the ridiculous."

It is with great joy that we are informed that Monsieur le Comte has now risen and is willing to grant us an audience. We are to take tea with him in the salon des fêtes, an enormous room whose main feature is a mahogany pulpit from a chapel, upon whose lectern the Count has a manuscript by Baudelaire in place of the antiphonary. A reverential hush precedes our host's entrance; d'Yturri has disappeared, presumably to add the final touches to the Count's face powder and ensure his moustache is suitably waxed.

A click of heels on the upper hall; the sound of a hissed argument between master and factotum; the insistent tap of an ebony cane upon the parapet; the coquettish odour of lilac perfume and there, at the top of the stairs. . .ecce homo!

Montesquiou strides down the stairs with d'Yturri hovering at his side, all traces of his former devotion to us now absent, in the presence of the sole object of his affection.

"Welcome, welcome to my home, humble seekers of the sublime!" The Count's black eyes flash under thick, arched eyebrows, complemented by a thick, Kaiser-like moustache with waxed, upturned edges. His face is ghostly white within a sheen of jet-black coiffured hair, his gaze powerful and serene as he scans the room like a battlefield. As we behold his attire, Mahomet's anecdote grows in resonance: we had expected the Count to appear in a suitably outrageous outfit for our first and only visit, but he has displayed absolute sartorial eccentricity by being clothed entirely in shades of grey: an iron-grey tail coat; mouse-grey gaiters; a pearl-grey waistcoat embroidered with chrysanthemums; a rare stone pinned to a dove-grey cravat and mauve-grey gloves.

"All this grey! Are you in mourning, Count?" asks a foolish, taffeta-clad siren among our number.

"Yes! For the dead leaves of autumn!" is the Count's dazzling riposte. After serving tea in delightful Japanese cups, Montesquiou seems eager to complete our guided tour of his abode. We begin with a visit to the study, an immense room with tall plinths lacquered a deep indigo, the coved ceiling covered in morocco leather and set with a circular piece of royal-blue silk embroidered with silver seraphim. Drawings by La Gandara and Helleu adorn the walls and the shelves are crammed with a bizarre assortment of curios and mementoes: here a Tanagra figurine; there a lock of Byron's hair in a lacquered Japanese casket.

In a glass case among the bookshelves is a collection of 36 letters from Paul Verlaine to the Count, which he has had bound in morocco leather. They are written on coarse hospital paper, pink prostitutes' cards or the back of wine-merchants' bills. Speaking eloquently of Verlaine's genius, Montesquiou is modest enough to omit mention of his own tireless support of the poverty stricken and disease-ridden poet, in whose final months was able to number the Count among his few sources of financial and spiritual help.

We now descend the stairs once more and are led to view the fountains in the courtyard where Montesquiou has had sycamores planted and oleanders placed in porcelain tubs. The fountains are switched on, prompting the Count to muse, "Fireworks, the flying rockets of which let fall their sparks to meet the silky and coralline bouquets of sensual laurel blossoms . . .one might call it a massacre of doves, their imaginary down mingling with these borrowed gems, these artificial petals. Sham flowers and false feathers, illusory rubies are absorbed into the broken smile of the horizon, which closes like the lips of a wound."

A discussion ensues, mostly conducted by the Count, on the superiority of artifice over reality. His brilliant words on this subject clearly close to his heart are far too lengthy to include here, but he concludes with an elegant axiom: "The imagination can provide a more than adequate substitute for the vulgar reality of actual experience."

"Ah, Gabriel, I am tired now!" sighs the Count. D'Yturri, absorbed in a reverie provoked by Montesquiou's musings, immediately springs to his side with a look of pained concern. "My dear Robert, I should like to put under your tired steps a carpet of thornless roses."

With that we are bid farewell by the exquisite pair and with cries of "Magician!" "Sublime entertainment!" and "He is indeed a Professor of Beauty!", our party descends the blue hydrangea-bordered steps to the gate, to exit once more to the lustreless paving stones of reality.

Enemas For Pleasure

OVER THE CENTURIES, the Englishman has developed a deep suspicion towards anything to do with his nether regions and, for the main part, rightly so. Not for him the unsightly effeminacy of the bidet, the unsavoury exhibitionism of the sauna or the degradation of the Parisian pissoir. All these Latin affectations are apt to make a man's blood run cold. Having said this, a fellow of vim and vigour should never be frightened of indulging in unfamiliar realms of hedonistic activity and it would be folly if we were to be too hasty in dismissing a procedure which, if administered judiciously, soberly and above all discreetly, is capable of raising not only one's eyebrows but also one's mental and aesthetic awareness.

In his quest for thrilling new experiences, the Anarcho-Dandy takes inspiration from JK Huysmans' seminal work *A Rebours* (or *Against Nature* as it is known in translation), a novel published in 1884 that chronicles the exotic, sensuous experimentations of a faded and effete nobleman, Duc Jean Floressas des Esseintes. Alienated by the vulgarity of modern life he immures himself in the self-imposed exile of his ancestral chateau and finally, having resorted to all manner of continental jiggery-pokery in an attempt to rejuvinate his flagging appetite for life and distance himself from the common herd, he happens upon the grand serendipity of 'the enema'. "On account of the ruinous condition of his stomach, he had never been able to take a serious interest in the art of cookery, but now he found himself working out recipes of a perverse epicurianism."

For a moderate outlay of cash and with the barest minimum of unpleasant bending, the modern day gent can also find himself dallying in the invigorating mysteries of funnel and tubing. To get started all one needs are the following easily obtained household requisites.

1. A Jacobean four-poster bed.
2. An ankle-length satin dressing gown.
3. A family-size kitchen funnel, icing syringe or purpose-made enema bag.
4. An eight-foot length of heavy-duty, industrial, large-gauge rubber tubing.
5. One bottle of Lafite-Rothschild 1980 and one glass.
6. A jar of 'Hatton's (Old Devil) Bottom Lubricant'.
7. One Philippino maid-servant (optional).
8. One pair of high-quality white cotton gloves.
9. A slim volume of Mallarmé.
10. One large kitchen jug.

You'll soon find there's no end to the vibrant combinations of ingredients you can try. Why not experiment with some of the fun-packed, life-affirming coctions below?

A. Purgative Enema

Pearce's *General Textbook of Nursing* suggests this delightful pre-BSE enema, for those hell-bent on bowel movement coupled with lasting brain damage. "The ox-bile enema containing 2–4 drachms of ox bile mixed with 4–8 ounces of starch mucilage or warm water" is guaranteed to gain you a reputation for fast moving, madcap party antics.

B. Montezuma's Banquet

As an early morning pick-me-up this one's pretty hard to beat, but beware: it is not for the faint trousered. You will need:

2–3 teaspoonsful of chilli powder
4 ounces of tequila
8 ounces of yerba maté
8 ounces of petroleum distillate
1 whole capsicum pepper (*as garnish*)

C. Voodoo Pooper-Scooper

A light tropical enema suitable for contemplative sunset gazing. Very conducive to beautiful thoughts.

4 ounces of white rum
4 ounces of dark rum
1 alligator tooth (ground)
5 drops of laudanum
8 ounces of corn oil
1 maraschino cherry

D. London Derrière

Ideal accompaniment to a chill winter's night. Best administered by one's maid-servant whilst listening to Rachmaninov.

4 ounces of dry London gin
6 ounces of pea soup
Tincture of Myrrh
2 ounces of cod liver oil
2 olives

THE WAY OF THE TROUSER

THE G&T CEREMONY

THE TEMPLE
OF DIONYSUS

PLEASING EXPERIMENTS WITH
G L O V E S

The Way of the Trouser

Fig. 1.
The Grand Pipemaster
exhibits his characteristic hauteur in response to a question regarding the unpleasantness of modern social mores.

BY THIS STAGE it wouldn't be too surprising if readers found themselves a trifle weary and dazed, with heads brimming full of notions related to social upheaval and self-improvement. A young man eager to embrace the principles of Chappism can sometimes find himself daunted by the commitment that a whole new ethical code entails. He may regard himself as unequal to the job and uncertain that he will be able to live up to such exacting standards. It is true that we have covered much ground in a very short space of time, and this may well be an appropriate point at which to take a few precious moments away from the ferment of revolutionary zeal and seek halcyon glades where a man might 'find himself'.

Now that you possess the skills and armoury that will ultimately lead to an earthly paradise, it would be well worth distancing ourselves from the world for a while and attempt to digest everything we have learned so far. Whilst concentration on the fundamental necessities of life, such as exquisite tailoring and sumptuous comestibles, is generally calculated to keep most men in a state of rude psychological health, there occasionally arises a need in a Chap to face himself in the most uncompromising of terms and attempt to unravel the nature of his very soul.

With this appetite in mind, a mystically inclined branch of the Confederacy of Anarcho-Dandyists has set up a training centre in a stately home ensconced in the midst of the Cotswolds. The Branch Dandian Sect, as they have come to be called, seek to cater to a gentleman's spiritual requirements and introduce him to the system of self-analysis and ethics that is know as the Way of the Trouser.

The centre is led by Hubert Distaff, a former haberdasher from Acton and the self-styled Grand Pipemaster. His stated aims are to probe the essential shallowness of human existence, and create a philosophy based on the incandescent superficiality of the world and the immutable perfection of finely-crafted legwear.

The first thing that acolytes are taught when they enter the portals of the Grand Lodge are the Three Principles of The Trouser. These are as follows.

1) Truth can only be discovered in the surface of things.

2) Appearing natural and unaffected is the profoundest feat of artifice known to man.

3) Man is born criminally innocent and must constantly strive to attain a state of pure corruption.

These will hold any young gent in good stead when he finds himself ready to return to the outside world. Many of our most skilled and dedicated *agents raconteurs* have at one time or another been pupils of the Grand Pipemaster and while it is perfectly possible to lead a life of secular Chappism, attending the Lodge, even for a brief weekend course, is highly recommended.

The regimen on offer at the Lodge is difficult to define, combining as it does aspects of religious retreat, Swiss finishing school, *fin de siècle* banquet and Limehouse opium den. But what is clear from the outset is that 'tourists' will not be tolerated. New Age 'hippies' and aged Californians who occasionally infiltrate the premises, entertaining notions of 'accessing primal energy' or 'finding the child within', are soon unearthed and unceremoniously ousted.

This vetting procedure commences as soon as the course begins. Novices are introduced to each other over fine malt whisky and extra-caffeinated coffee. In the very first meeting they are invited to 'walk the Telegraph'. Cocky beginners may imagine it a simple matter to walk across the unfolded pages of this daily newspaper without crumpling its delicate leaves, but one attempt is enough to confirm that all initiates lack the requisite dash to perambulate the

Fig. 2.
Walking the Telegraph.
A sturdy-hearted fellow attempts to walk upon a daily newspaper without making any impression on its dainty pages.

journal without doing unsightly damage to headline and sports page alike. "When you can walk the Telegraph and leave no trace of your passing," intones the Grand Pipemaster, "then you will be ready to leave this place and enter the outside world."

Suitably chastened, the novitiate set to work to prove themselves worthy of the Pipemaster's trust. Nights are spent memorising intricate cocktail recipes, perfecting the creases in serge trouser legs and destroying myriad brain-cells through the use of powerful hallucinogens.

The next morning, the Pipemaster speaks. "Contemplate, my children, the reassuring practicality of the humble briar, the baroque assertiveness of the meerschaum, the serpentine grace of the calabash and the cheeky immoderacy of the churchwarden. Surely human existence is akin to the fleeting perfume that rises from an amply-stuffed bowl of navy shag."

Rarely has the Chap's philosophy been stated with such clarity.

"The Way of the Trouser is a way of peace, a way of harmony, but also a way of strength. Let us judge our fellow man by the strength of his handshake, the quality of his cufflinks and the uncompromising nature of his trouser creases."

Thoroughly inspired, the following days are dedicated to esoteric tasks such as picking up soup tureens with both wrists, buffing up one's bare feet with boot polish (finding the inner brogue) and contemplating the re-introduction of the antimacassar as a staple of modern interior design. It might seem difficult for novices to fathom precisely what they are gaining from such activities, but the shrewd knowingness of the Grand Pipemaster must be trusted. He is simply breaking down ingrained social mores and enabling his students to release themselves from the hideous conventions of modern life. Once this is accomplished he will be able to rebuild them as men of stoic corsetry, impeccable courteousness and loose morals.

'De-programming' is usually achieved by the end of the first week, but building the perfect *agent raconteur* is likely to take somewhat longer. Every seven days students are once again invited to 'walk the Telegraph', and as the fleetness of their calf-skin clad feet improves, they begin to leave less and less of an impression on its surface. Such nimbleness of foot will be invaluable in the outside world when indulging in the rigours of Anarcho-Dandyist action.

Again the Pipemaster speaks. "You must see the world through a glass of single malt darkly. When you leave this place, let your wine merchant be your only spiritual adviser. Why swim with dolphins, when you can swim with amphetamines?"

All are overcome at such insight.

By week 15, the callow initiates have been miraculously transformed from ill-hewn boys to straight-backed fops of pasty-faced grandeur. They have cast aside ridiculous ideas regarding 'discovering the deepest recesses of the subconcious self' and instead pass their days ensuring that their shirt cuffs are stiffened with precisely the correct amount of starch and that the gin in their martinis is never tainted by the addition of too much vermouth. They have come to realise that the sparkling and light-soaked surface of things is so much more moving and beautiful than the crepuscular netherworld of a man's psyche. Appearance is truth, shallowness is profundity and superficiality is king.

Pleasing Experiments with Gloves

AS WE HAVE seen with the enema, sensual experimentation can be health giving and a thoroughly invigorating practice for a Chap to dabble in once in a while. What is less well-known is that a disciplined investigation into decadent abandon can also provide a jolly decent workout for a man's spiritual side too. A man should never find himself too busy to create space in his life to allow his senses to roam freely, like the noble wildebeest migrating across the vast plains of the Serengeti.

Flirting with perfume, incense, precious stones and the intoxicating words of the poets is something of a dandy tradition, but the Anarcho-Dandy should be prepared to seek out and discover new succulent groves and halcyon glades in which to frolic with the nymphs and dryads of spiritual ecstasy. His area of enquiry should have one limit and that is the outer bounds of his imagination.

The quest for enlightenment need not always involve rare unctions, trips to exotic locations, weeks of preparation and the assistance of shamans and yogis. Household objects traditionally unassociated with the search for inner truth can, with a modicum of ingenuity and the flame of inspiration, be sequestered for use too. Here we demonstrate the fact, with various pleasing experiments that may be performed with nothing more complicated than the humble glove.

If the eyes are the windows to the soul, then the hands are the antennae and the conduit through which it restlessly searches for truth. What better way for a gentleman to explore the mysteries of his own shallowness than through those objects specifically designed to protect his refined digits from the detritus of the outside world. Gloves come in a bewildering array of styles and materials and should be selected depending on the particular ecstatic state one wishes to achieve. This is not an exact science and a beginner should learn to trust his intuition in such matters.

Fig. 1

EXPERIMENT 1
Getting One's Fingers Burnt

Retire to a dimly lit salon, preferably during the winter months, and try out this symbolically charged experiment. Lightly douse the ends of your gloved fingers with lighter fuel, recline into the depths of your favourite smoking chair and ignite (Fig.1). The flames from your finger tips will dance merrily before your eyes, conjuring up untold landscapes, forgotten faces and pagan ritual. Long associated with religious symbolism, the purifying tongues of fire will wash away your sins and purify you in readiness for the week of debauchery and excess that surely lies ahead.

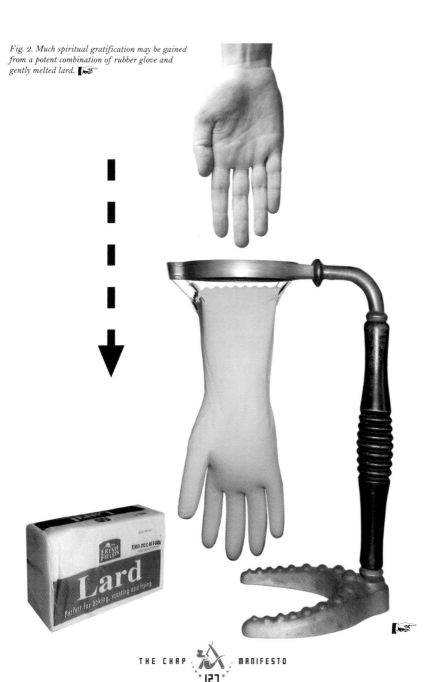

Fig. 2. Much spiritual gratification may be gained from a potent combination of rubber glove and gently melted lard. 👉

Experiment 2
The Heady Exuberance of Rubber and Lard

The chances are that a pair of domestic rubber gloves have been lurking in your kitchen cupboard for quite some time. Due to a complete abhorrence of cooking and the domestic chores associated with such activity, you will only be dimly aware of the fact, but go on, have a look under that sink, you'll be surprised what you find.

Fish out one glove, it is important that it is free from punctures, and suspend it in the manner shown in Fig. 2. At the same time, gently heat a block of lard in a saucepan. When barely melted and pleasantly warm to the touch, pour the lard into the glove. You now have the equivalent of a flotation tank for the digital extremities. Roll up your sleeve and feel the amniotic tide rising up your fingers. The womb beckons and you will gradually sense that the earth mother herself is giving you succour.

Experiment 3
The Waft of an Angel's Wings

Associating with the ladies can have numerous benefits, but chief among them is the ready availability of sundry hand garments with which to experiment. Sit firmly in an upright dining chair and ask your ladylove to thrash the air before your face with one of her long satin evening gloves. The whole point of this experiment is that the glove never actually makes contact (Fig. 3). The essence is in the waft of perfumed air as it passes a fraction of an inch from your face. The frisson gained from the Angel's Wing is akin to that experienced by art lovers when observing the gap between the fingers of God and Adam on the ceiling of the Sistine Chapel.

Fig. 3

The G&T Ceremony

THERE ARE FEW BALMS more efficacious in the restoration of a fellow's bruised psyche than the immoderate consumption of gin. An essential ingredient in the classic dry martini, gin is less an alcoholic beverage and more a way of life. Therefore, it should come as no surprise that throughout the ages highly involved rituals have evolved in association with this juniper berry elixir. One of the best documented of these is the ancient and decorative G&T ceremony.

Step 1. **The Reciting of the Botanicals**

The aromatic, botanical ingredients that give gin its distinctive flavour are recited from memory prior to the breaking of the seal.

Step 2. **The Opening & Pouring of the Gin**

Hushed reverence and a slight intake of breath as the seal is broken and the heady aroma of the newly opened bottle pervades the room.

Step 3. **The Exposition of the Tonic**

The chilled tonic is held aloft in a cut-glass jug so that all may marvel at its sparkling beauty. Recite, "Behold quinine – mighty tonic of the Gods."

Step 4. **The Pouring of the Tonic**

The Indian tonic water mingles seductively with the gin and all recite, "Cast ye out all Slimline usurpers. Curse ye substitutes, Oh Schweppes."

Step 5. The Blessing of the Lemon

A brief paeon to the lemon tree for its citric bounty. The whole room subsides into awe at the unutterable loveliness of the sentiments expressed.

Step 6. The Cutting of the Lemon

The lemon should be tackled with vigour and aplomb. The slicing is regarded as a firm indication of a man's virility.

Step 7. The Dunking of the Lemon

The lemon is dunked ceremoniously three times before being allowed to gently glide afloat. All recite: "Verily the drought hath almost ended."

Step 8: The Addition of the Ice & the Quaff

Ice, made from the finest spring water, should be added last to avoid over diluting the sacred spirit. A mighty quaff should follow without delay.

TOWARDS THE LAPIS LAZULI DAWN

CHAPPIST PROPAGANDA

MOBILE PHONE AMNESTY ■ **LETTERS** ■ **SIGNING OFF**

Agit-Fop

A SELECTION OF CHAPPIST stickers, which can be discreetly placed in areas where the vulgaroise tend to congregate, such as office buildings, fast food outlets and department stores.

YOU ARE ENTERING A DOFFING ZONE

ALL PROPER TEA IS BEST.

VANITY IS ALL

COURTESY IS CONTAGIOUS

Epistolary Warfare

A CLEVERLY-WORDED LETTER to the right person can have as much effect on an organisation as a brick thrown through its window. Here are some suggested letters that chumrades can write to protest against anti-Chappist activities.

To: The Public Relations Officer,
Berkshire Division,
McDonald's plc.

Sir,

I notice with interest that you have added a cafeteria to all your public lavatories. I realise that because the lavatories are provided gratis they have to be funded in some way, but I must protest at the quality of the food being served in the attached cafeterias. The combination of cheap beef derivatives, starchy white buns and 'French fries' merely serves to exacerbate the unpleasant odours naturally present in any public lavatory, to the point where the pong in some of the larger branches is almost unbearable.

Furthermore, I fail to understand why the cafeteria has to be so disproportionately large compared to the toilet facilities themselves. Surely the ratio of lavatory:feeding area should be reversed, so that one doesn't have to wait too long to perform one's ablutions when in a hurry?

Yours,
Sir Peregrine Woolstolencraft

To: The Station Supervisor,
Torquay Railway Station,
Devon

Sir,

I recently witnessed a horrible crime at your station. A clearly distressed young man was bein[g] mugged by another fellow. Fortunately I have a natural aptitude for criminal detection and I memorised his face.

The thief was aged around 40, with a pasty grey face that displayed signs of weariness and genera[l] dissatisfaction with life. He was wearing a bogus uniform of your station platform staff and the amou[nt] he was demanding of his victim was exactly £10.

I have witnessed similar crimes at various stations around the country, always for the same amount. I think it is time you put some serious thought to this matter, perhaps employing special members of staff to deal with these criminals.

Yours,
The Marquis of Lansdowne (disgraced)

To: The Manager,
Salford Internet Cafe,
High Street,
Salford

Sir,

On a recent perambulation past your establishment, I was tempted by the sign in the window that read 'Chat Rooms'. I was rather in the mood for a chat with someone, so I entered the building and paid the requested one pound. Unfortunately, my attempts to engage any of the other clients in conversation proved entirely fruitless. The first fellow I approached, who sported an unfeasibly large knapsack decorated with flags representing one of the former colonies, expressed open vexation at my interruption. He was fixated on a species of television screen, while fiddling about with an electric typewriter on the table he was sitting at.

As I looked about the Cafe, I noticed with alarm that all the customers were watching television and operating typewriters. May I suggest to you, Sir, that were you to remove all these electronic devices, the customers may then feel more inclined to actually engage in conversation with each other. Your advertised 'Chat Rooms' might then become a reality.

Yours,
Brigadier Henry St Wittermaster, QC

To: Personnel Manager
Head Office,
Starbucks UK

Sir,

A recent visit to one of your establishments caused me some consternation. After waiting at a table without being served, I approached the service counter and requested a pot of Earl Grey tea and a round of cucumber sandwiches, before returning to my table.

Presently I was called by the rather discourteous member of your staff who informed me that my tea was ready. The requested pot of Earl Grey was nowhere to be seen; instead I was handed a polystyrene cup of hot water with a round tea bag floating in it. "And what of the cucumber sandwiches?" I asked the young cub that I had no mate, we don't do them," came the insolent reply. "How about a ciabatta with Chicken Tikka Masala and roasted vegetables?" I informed the young cub that I had no appetite for the contents of someone's dustbin in a sandwich, and that I neither knew nor wished to know what ungodly thing is a ciabatta.

I shall not be returning to any branches of Starbucks unless you can improve the quality of service and employ staff who understand the meaning of the word.

Yours,
Lord Charles Bamberston-Caerphilly

Mobile Phone Amnesty

AS WE DRAW towards the close of this manifesto, the CAD feels compelled to make some gesture of compassion and magnanimity towards those lost souls who find themselves trapped in lives weighed down by consumerism and vulgarity.

Our campaign to rid the streets and public places of that organ of disharmony, the mobile phone, is set to show great advances in the coming years, but now in a mood of conciliation and with a sincere desire to help mobophiles turn their backs on their sordid pasts, the CAD is pleased to announce a mobile phone amnesty. Members of the benighted hoi polloi are encouraged to surrender their ignoble instruments of shame, either by turning them in to the proper authorities or by posting them to the CAD HQ. All horns of misery received are melted down and cast into figurines of Barbey D'Aurevilly, proceeds from whose sales will be channelled back into Anarcho-Dandyist activism. But rest assured that out on the street the CAD will continue its campaign of random acts of common courtesy with renewed vigour, assuring that the powers of unseemliness and discord are crushed underfoot like so many gastropods beneath the mud-clogged boot of a particularly vindictive gardener.

A Final Call to Charms

CHAPPISM, ALTHOUGH A FRINGE MOVEMENT (or, more accurately, a side parting movement) at present, is steadily growing. Our number may be small, but our might is enormous. Across the land, Anarcho–Dandyist cells are gradually being formed. Collectives of besuited men with immaculate kid gloves, moleskin waistcoats and sharp creases in their trousers are gathering in dimly lit taverns to discuss the future.

They see a future where Chappism ultimately destroys the tyranny of the vulgaroisie, and installs the pasty-faced fop in his rightful place as the icon of the age. They see a world in which Chappism, by controlling the means of production, education and the family, creates a society in which poetry, beautiful thoughts and dazzling cufflinks rule the day. A world where the young will not have to worry about ISAs, TESSAs and Personal Equity Plans, but can concentrate exclusively on Personal Grooming Plans.

We urge you to apply the techniques we have suggested in our humble tome to your every activity, to ensure that the vulgaroisie is brought to its knees, and that all nastiness and rudery is pushed aside in the name of Chappism. Every little gesture that flies in the face of neo–vulgarity can help the Tweed Revolution.

Stroll with us along the tree-lined boulevards of our quest for a better world, pausing occasionally to adjust your immaculate buttonhole, or to inhale the intoxicating perfume of the lilies that will one day grace the borders of every street, in every town, in every country. Chumrades, we urge you to be those very lilies.

Gustav Temple
& Vic Darkwood

Messrs Temple and Darkwood are pleased to acknowledge the help of the following chumrades in the creation of this manifesto:

Susan Smith and Meg Davis at MBA, Tony Lyons and everyone at M2,
Andy Miller and Clive Priddle at 4th Estate,
Liam Bailey, Jake Clark, Robin Dutt, Stephan Fowler, Liz Harris,
Tim O'Sullivan, Mark Pawson, David Saxby,
Ted Sedman and Cindy Sullivan